Introduction

Our world is a small and fragile planet, less than 8,000 miles in diameter. Nearly three-quarters of the Earth is covered by the oceans, leaving us just 29 per cent of land surface on which to live and grow most of our food.

Every minute of the day and night, some 274 babies are born around the world (395,000 babies every 24 hours). This birth rate adds another 93,000,000 people to the human population each year.

As more and more people demand more and more land for development, the wild places become smaller and fewer. The destruction of habitats means that many species of plants and animals are threatened with extinction. Poachers kill animals to meet the demands of tourists or to satisfy ancient superstitions. Pollution of the air, soil, rivers and oceans affect us all to a greater or lesser degree and the outlook can seem rather grim.

In all this gloom, there is one particular ray of hope shining through – this is the increasing interest that people like you are showing in world environmental problems. After all, it will be 'your' world before long, so you need to understand some of the problems facing the world as humanity approaches the twenty-first century. Perhaps your generation will be the first to start taking better care of Planet Earth.

Cyril Littlewood MBE, OGA
Founder & Director,
Young People's Trust for the Environment
& Nature Conservation (YPTENC)

FREE MEMBERSHIP
The Young People's Trust for the Environment & Nature Conservation (YPTENC)

If you are aged 16 or under, you can become a member of the **YPTENC** without charge and make full use of the Trust's free Information Service.

The **Information Service** can provide you with useful and informative factsheets on wildlife, endangered species and environmental problems (please include a stamped, self-addressed envelope to receive your answer).

The Trust also operates a busy **School Lecture Service** covering all age ranges and a wide variety of topics.

Another aspect of the Trust's work are the residential **Environmental Discovery Courses** for children aged 9 to 16 that it runs on the Dorset coast.

Please send for details of membership or our services to schools to:
Cyril Littlewood MBE, OGA,
Founder & Director
YPTENC, 8 Leapale Road, Guildford,
Surrey GU1 4JX
Telephone: 01483 39600
Fax: 01483 301992

THE CHANGING WORLD

JUNGLES & RAINFORESTS

JOHN A. BURTON

DRAGON'S WORLD

CHILDREN'S BOOKS

Code of Safety

Most of the habitats described in this series are dangerous because they are at the extremes of how our world works. They are not places you should visit without preparation or without a qualified guide. You should take suitable equipment and wear the right clothing for the environment. Take a map and a compass on all trips and learn how to use them properly. If you should find yourself in such a place through an accident, you will find some tips on how to survive there on page 67.

- **Before you go on a trip**, plan your route. **Always** tell an adult where you are going and when you expect to return.
- **Always go with a friend**, and preferably go as a party of four, which is a safe minimum number. If possible, go with at least one adult whom you trust – ideally someone who knows the area and the subject you are studying.
- **Ask permission** before going on to private property.
- **Leave gates closed or open** depending on how you find them. Keep off crops and avoid damaging soils, plants, animals, fences, walls and gates.
- **Take your litter home** or dispose of it properly.
- **Remember** that many plants and animals, and their homes and habitats, are protected by law.
- **Ask your parents** not to light fires except in an emergency.
- **Beware of natural hazards** such as slippery slopes, crumbling cliffs, loose rocks, rotten tree trunks and branches, soft mud, deep water, swift currents and tides.
- **Beware of poisonous berries**, plants and animals: if you are not sure, don't touch them.
- Remember: **if in doubt, always play safe.**

Picture Credits

Alessandro Bartolozzi: 12/13. Bernard Thornton Artists: 6/7, 8/9, 10/11, 14, 16/17, 42/43, 46/47, 56/57 (Jim Channell); 28, 54 (George Fryer); 44, 52/53 (Robert Morton); 18/19, 30/31, 40/41 (Tim Hayward); 58/59 (Colin Newman); 48/49, 50/51, 64/65 (David Thelwell). Hutchison Library: 66 (Edward Parker). Kevin Madison: 62/63; 66. Debbie Maizels: 20/21; 36. Oxford Illustrators: 24/25; 26/27; 32/33; 34/35; 38/39. Mike Saunders: 20/21. Science Photo Library: 46/47 (Dr Morley Read); back cover, endpapers, 1 (© Tom Van Sant, Geosphere Project, Santa Monica). Activity pictures by Mr Gay Galsworthy.

Dragon's World Ltd
Limpsfield
Surrey RH8 0DY
Great Britain

First published by Dragon's World Ltd, 1996

© Dragon's World Ltd, 1996
© Text John Burton, 1996
© Illustrations by specific artists, 1996

Editor	Diana Briscoe
Series Editor	Steve Parker
Designer	Martyn Foote
Art Director	John Strange
Design Assistants	Karen Ferguson
	Victoria Furbisher
DTP Manager	Michael Burgess
Editorial Director	Pippa Rubinstein

British Library Cataloguing in Publication Data
The catalogue record for this book is available from the British Library.

ISBN 1 85028 384 2

Typeset by Dragon's World Ltd in Garamond, Caslon 540 and Frutiger.
Printed in Italy

Contents

The Changing World of
Jungles and Rainforests

Our world, planet Earth, has never been still since it first formed – 4,600 million years ago. It goes around the Sun once each year, to bring the changing seasons. It spins like a top once each day, causing the cycle of day and night. Our close companion, the Moon, circles the Earth and produces the rise and fall of the ocean tides. The weather alters endlessly, too. Winds blow, water ripples into waves, clouds drift, rain falls and storms brew. Land and sea are heated daily by the Sun, and cool or freeze at night.

Living on the Earth, we notice these changes on different time scales. First and fastest is our own experience of passing time, as seconds merge into minutes and hours. We move about, eat and drink, learn and play, rest and sleep. Animals do many of these activities, too.

Second is the longer, slower time scale of months and years. Many plants grow and change over these longer time periods. Return to a natural place after many years, and you see how some of the trees have grown, while others have died and disappeared.

Third is the very long, very slow time scale lasting hundreds, thousands and millions of years. The Earth itself changes over these immense periods. New mountains thrust up; others wear down. Rivers alter their course. One sea fills with sediments, but huge earth movements and continental drift create another sea elsewhere.

The *CHANGING WORLD* series describes and explains these events – from the immense time span of lands and oceans, to the shorter changes among trees and flowers, to the daily lives of ourselves and other animals. Each book selects one feature or habitat of nature, to reveal in detail. Here you can read how wet *JUNGLES AND RAINFORESTS* really are, and how they are home to the richest variety of plants and animals on our planet, from massive trees and shapely orchids, to sparkling butterflies, chattering parrots and monkeys, and the big cats.

4

MORE, AND MORE, AND ...

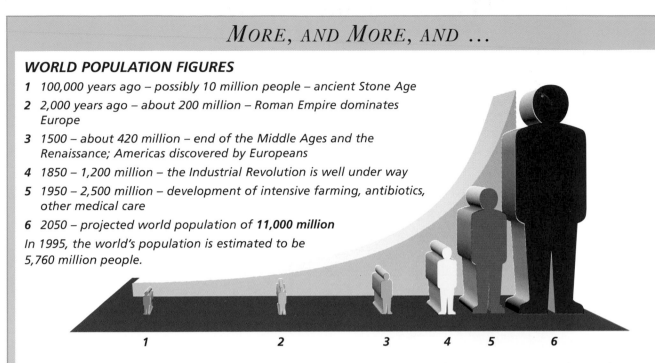

WORLD POPULATION FIGURES

1 *100,000 years ago – possibly 10 million people – ancient Stone Age*

2 *2,000 years ago – about 200 million – Roman Empire dominates Europe*

3 *1500 – about 420 million – end of the Middle Ages and the Renaissance; Americas discovered by Europeans*

4 *1850 – 1,200 million – the Industrial Revolution is well under way*

5 *1950 – 2,500 million – development of intensive farming, antibiotics, other medical care*

6 *2050 – projected world population of **11,000 million***

In 1995, the world's population is estimated to be 5,760 million people.

The most numerous large animal on Earth, by many millions, is the human. Our numbers have increased steadily from the start of civilization about 10,000 years ago speeded by advances in public health and hygiene, the Industrial Revolution, petrol and diesel engines, better farming and better medical care.

However, this massive growth in humanity means that almost half the world's people suffer from hunger, poverty and disease. The animals and plants who share our planet also suffer. As we expand our territory, their natural areas shrink ever faster. We probably destroy one species of plant or animal every week.

However, there is another type of change affecting our world. It is the huge and ever-increasing number of humans on the planet. The *CHANGING WORLD* series shows how we have completely altered vast areas – to grow foods, put up homes and other buildings, mine metals and minerals, manufacture goods and gadgets from pencils to washing machines, travel in cars, trains and planes, and generally carry on with our modern lives.

This type of change is causing immense damage.

We take over natural lands and wild places, forcing plants and animals into ever smaller areas. Some of them disappear for ever. We produce all kinds of rubbish, refuse, poisons and pollution.

However, there is hope. More people are becoming aware of the problems. They want to stop the damage, to save our planet, and to plan for a brighter future. The *CHANGING WORLD* series shows how we can all help. We owe it to our Earth, and to its millions of plants, animals and other living things, to make a change for the better.

What is a 'Jungle'?

The word 'jungle' comes from the Hindi word *jangal*. This really means a 'desert' or 'waste land'. During the days when India was part of the British Empire, the word was used by British people to describe the dry scrubland habitats in many parts of India, because there was no similar word in the English language at the time.

However, gradually the word changed to mean forests, and in particular, tropical forests. (A similar change had already happened to the word *forest*. Long ago, it meant 'a wilderness, waste land or unenclosed land'. Gradually it changed to denote a large wooded area. It is still used today for places like the New Forest – much of which is not woodland, but heathland!)

In recent times the terms 'jungle' and 'rainforest' have been used to describe a wide range of usually tropical forests. Strictly speaking, rainforests are areas where the trees are mostly more than

Cloud forests
As you go higher up a mountain, conditions become cooler. But the mist, fog and clouds that shroud the slopes provide plentiful water. Montane or cloud forests grow in these areas, with tall trees and huge plants such as giant lobelias and giant ragworts.

Island forests
Some of the wettest forests in the world are the hills and mountains on ocean islands, such as the Solomon Islands near Papua New Guinea and the Hawaiian Islands in the Pacific. Each island has its unique wildlife, especially butterflies and birds.

Gallery or riverine forests
These grow along the banks of rivers and around the edges of flooded areas. The trees must cope with their soil being flooded for several weeks each year. As the waters recede during the dry season, the forest is often left as a line or edge.

6

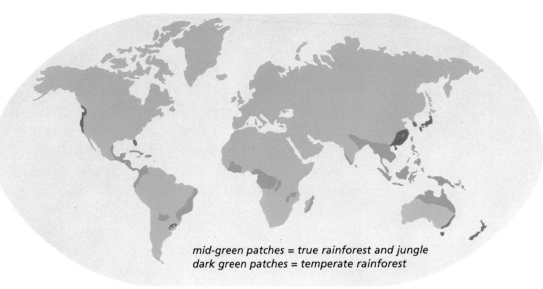

Rainforests of the world
This map shows the main areas of true rainforest and temperate rainforest. They cover less than one-twentieth of the world's land surface. Yet they are the richest areas in the world for wildlife – home to three-quarters of all known kinds (species) of plants and animals.

mid-green patches = true rainforest and jungle
dark green patches = temperate rainforest

30 metres high, they are deciduous (their leaves fall at a particular season) and there is high rainfall. There are also lots of creepers and lianas, as well as numerous epiphytes – plants growing not on the ground but high in the trees, such as orchids, air plants and bromeliads. Rainforests occur both in tropical and temperate regions. So the technically correct term for what are popularly called jungles or rainforests is 'tropical moist forests'.

The animals of these forests are incredibly numerous and diverse, from tiny, brightly coloured arrow-poison frogs to huge gorillas, giant anacondas and boas, flying squirrels and a breathtaking array of brilliantly coloured birds and butterflies.

Rhododendron forests
Rhododendrons are well known in many parts of the world as garden plants. Yet their natural home is the rainy slopes of the Himalaya Mountains, which are covered with huge forests of them. The giant rhododendron grows up to 25 m tall.

THE LIVING WEIGHT

The weight of living and ex-living matter (plants and animals) in a habitat is called the biomass. In a typical conifer forest (right), half the biomass is below ground in the soil, as dead leaves and rotting plants. In a tropical rainforest (left), the total biomass is ten times more, and almost all is above ground, as trees.

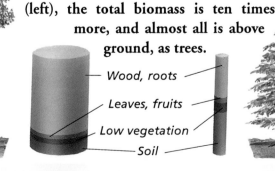

Wood, roots
Leaves, fruits
Low vegetation
Soil

Deep in the Jungle

In a natural mature rainforest, it is surprisingly gloomy and strangely quiet. The leaves and branches of the canopy, far above, cut out most of the light. The trees are often huge, 45-55 metres, but sometimes over 80 metres. Several species have vast buttresses stretching out around the lower part of the tree, in order to help support the immense weight of their boughs, leaves and fruits high above.

The ground vegetation is rather sparse. Between the trees is a thick carpet or litter of decaying leaves. The majority of the smaller plants are not small flowers or herbs, but tree seedlings trying to grow. Lianas and vines are often very large, with woody stems twisting around the tree trunks and hanging under the canopy.

Many types of flowers and other plants grow in the rainforest – but not in the soil on the ground. They live high on the boughs and trunks of the tall trees, nearer the vital light. They include ferns, orchids and bromeliads.

Some of the most secretive yet spectacular forest inhabitants are the big cats. Lions once lived across Africa, the Middle East and Asia. Now they survive in large numbers only in Africa – and in the small Gir Forest in north-western India. This is home to the last surviving groups of Asian lions. They live in the more open forest or *jangal* and are protected by law. Their big-cat cousins, the tigers, live in denser forests and rainforests. Big cats sometimes come into conflict with villagers, killing their cattle and other livestock. In the last fifty years, both Asian lions and tigers have become very rare.

What Makes a Rainforest?

The main condition needed for a rainforest is – rain. In general, the average rainfall must be at least 2,000 millimetres (2 metres) each year, and this should be spread out over most of the year. This compares with the rainfall in London, which averages 590 millimetres each year, and New York, which has about 1,100 millimetres of rain yearly. Tropical rainforests have temperatures which are high and vary little, usually between 20° and 28°C all year. Temperate rainforests are generally cooler, around 10°C in winter and up to 25°C in summer.

The combination of moisture and warmth, especially in the tropical rainforests, means that the growing conditions for living are near ideal. The diversity of plant life, with abundant flowers, fruits, seeds, berries, nuts and foliage, provides food for a huge range of animals.

The animals also benefit from the tropical conditions of heat, light and moisture. Most small animals are 'cold-blooded', which means that they cannot control their body temperature in the way

Wet winds over Borneo
Rainforests and jungles grow where there is plenty of rain. This usually happens where winds have blown over an ocean and picked up lots of water vapour, then blow over land. The vapour condenses into tiny droplets that form clouds, then larger drops that fall as rain. The island of Borneo in South-East Asia has these conditions. It is also very hilly, so much of the forest still survives, rather than being cleared for farming.

Borneo lies on the Equator and so is hot all year round.

Water vapour in cooled air condenses as it rises over hills, and falls as rain.

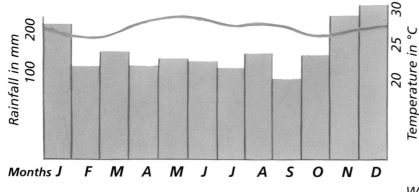

Rainfall in mm 100 200

Temperature in °C 20 25 30

Months J F M A M J J A S O N D

Temperature and rainfall
The temperature in most parts of lowland Borneo varies little through the year, being around 26–28°C. Of course, it is cooler in the higher hills and mountains. The rainfall totals about 2,600 millimetres and is highest from November to March. There are no dry months. In the hills, there are few dry days.

Winds blow mainly from south during middle of year (July).

Narrow coastal plain supports some farming.

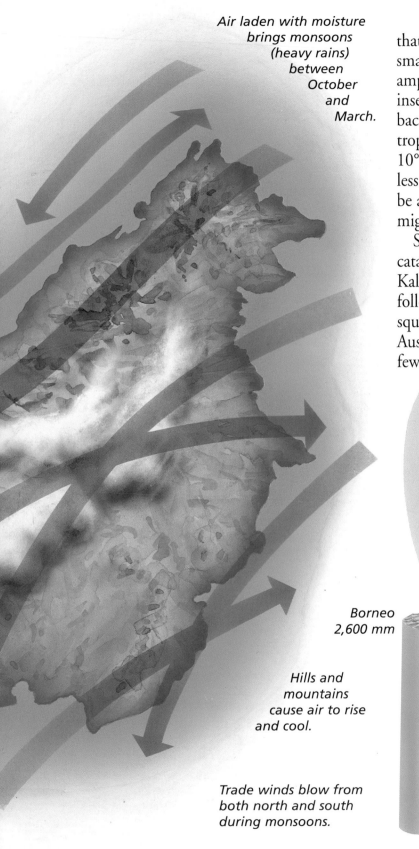

Air laden with moisture brings monsoons (heavy rains) between October and March.

that 'warm-blooded' birds and mammals can. So small vertebrates (animals with backbones) such as amphibians, reptiles and fish, and the spiders, insects and other invertebrates (beasts without backbones), all occur in far greater variety in the tropics. The temperature rarely drops below about 10°C, even at night. As the food supply is more or less constant throughout the year, the animals can be active all year, too. Few creatures hibernate or migrate long distances away from the forest.

Surprisingly, tropical forests can sometimes suffer catastrophically from drought. In 1982-3 in eastern Kalimantan, on the island of Borneo, a drought was followed by a fire which devastated about 33,000 square kilometres – an area larger than Belgium or Austria. However, some trees did survive. After a few years, plants and animals were thriving again.

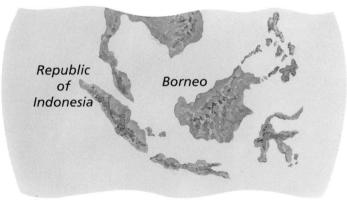

Republic of Indonesia

Borneo

Hills and mountains cause air to rise and cool.

Borneo
2,600 mm

New York
1,100 mm

London
590 mm

Warm and wet
Borneo is one of the large islands of South-East Asia (above). Its annual rainfall is four times that of a city such as London. There are also many fewer dry days, even on the lowlands, perhaps only 30 each year.

Trade winds blow from both north and south during monsoons.

11

Why Do We Need Jungles?

Jungles and rainforests have great effects on the world's atmosphere and climate. Their trees, flowers and other plants carry out the process of photosynthesis, catching light energy in their leaves and using it to live and grow. As they do so, they take in the gas carbon dioxide and give out the gas oxygen. This is the opposite of what we and other animals do when we breathe, using up oxygen and giving out carbon dioxide. So the mass of plant life in rainforests helps to keep the air fresh and topped up with oxygen. It also gets rid of carbon dioxide, which is poisonous if too plentiful.

Rainforests also work as giant 'sponges'. An area covered with forest not only attracts moisture, particularly at night, in the form of mists and rain. It also holds that water, mainly in plants and soil.

Oxygen used by breathing and burning.

Carbon dioxide produced by breathing and burning.

Keeping air fresh
Rainforest areas help to maintain the natural balance of gases in the atmosphere. They also help to counteract the harmful extra greenhouse gases that humans produce, especially in cities. Their main effects are on the gases oxygen and carbon dioxide, and also on water vapour.

Oxygen produced by photosynthesis, carbon dioxide used for photosynthesis.

Water eventually drains into the sea, evaporates as water vapour, rises and condenses into clouds, and falls on rainforest again, as part of the water cycle.

Leaves, wood and soil hold water like a giant sponge.

INCREDIBLE DIVERSITY

In a square kilometre of typical temperate deciduous woodland in North America or Europe, you might find: 10 main tree species (green), 100 species of flowers and other plants (orange), and 1,000 small animal species such as worms and insects, plus 100 larger animal species such as birds and mammals (pink).

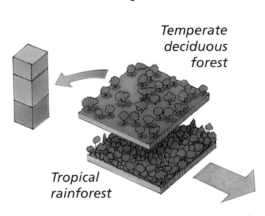

Temperate deciduous forest

Tropical rainforest

In a square kilometre of tropical rainforest, all these numbers would be 100 times more, even 1,000 times more, especially those for flowers and insects.

Some of the water trickles slowly into the rivers and streams, while the rest is given off as water vapour, mainly during the day-time. So rainforests protect their soil from being washed away by this sponge effect. They also release moisture slowly and steadily into the atmosphere, affecting cloud and weather patterns for thousands of kilometres.

The tropical rainforests are fantastic centres of living variety, or biodiversity. Thousands of species of plants live in an area that, in a cooler part of the world, would have only a few hundred species. Myriad insects feed on them, and in turn fall prey

'Lungs of the world'
Rainforests are sometimes called the 'lungs of the world'. Human and animal lungs breathe in oxygen (O_2) and breathe out carbon dioxide (CO_2). Jungles do the reverse, their plants taking in carbon dioxide and giving out oxygen.

O_2 CO_2

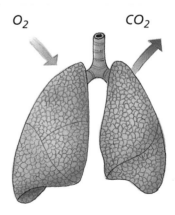

to an astonishing variety of birds, bats and other animals. This biodiversity still amazes scientists. Many now believe that there are at least 25 million different types of plants and animals on Earth – mostly in rainforests, and still unknown to science.

Seasons in the Rainforests

Not all rainforests are in the hot tropics. There are smaller patches of rainforests in temperate lands such as southern Australia, New Zealand, western North America and southern South America. On the South Island of New Zealand, the temperate rainforest is concentrated on the windward side of the island. The annual average rainfall here is 2,500 millimetres each year and the temperatures vary from about 10°C in winter to 25°C in summer. This forest is termed 'sub-Antarctic' and is based on species of southern beech trees, *Nothofagus*, especially the red beech *Nothofagus fusca* and the silver beech *Nothofagus menziesii*. The trees cloak the foothills and higher slopes of the mountains in the south-west of the island. Much of the area is now protected as a nature reserve and national park.

Wet winds
The prevailing winds blowing from the north-west on to New Zealand's South Island are loaded with water vapour. As they move over land and rise up the mountains, they cool and drop the water as rain.

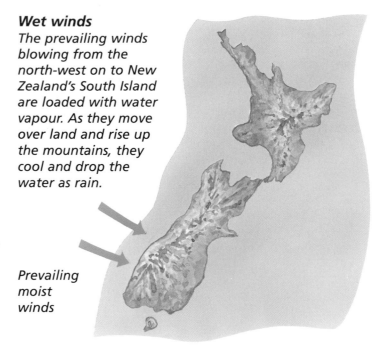

Prevailing moist winds

In the past, New Zealand's North Island had some sub-tropical rainforest, but this has suffered the same fate as huge areas of tropical rainforest across the middle of the world. It has mostly been cleared for farm land, for growing crops and raising animals. Roads, factories and towns also use up the once-wild land. As in many other parts of the world, the main remnants of the North Island's rainforest are in the hills and mountains, where the land is too steep or rocky for agriculture.

Winter and summer
Trees that shed their leaves in one season, usually autumn or the dry season, are termed deciduous. The red beech and silver beech of New Zealand are evergreen. The leaves do not last for ever – they live for three or four years. They are lost in small numbers through most of the year. So the trees may look thinly leaved at certain times, but they are never completely bare.

Water Everywhere!

All plants need water. They suck it in through their roots and pass it up their stems and into their leaves. The water carries minerals and nutrients from the soil to the leaves, for growth. Pure water then evaporates from the leaves as invisible water vapour, given off into the air. You can show the stages of this process using ordinary household plants. In the rainforest, there is so much moisture, that plant growth is greatly encouraged. Also the air is made very humid with the water vapour given off by plants.

1 *Choose a potted houseplant with plenty of green leaves, which you can pretend is in a jungle. You also need a large clear plastic bag and string. Water the soil in the pot well.*

1 *A stick of celery can substitute for the fleshy, succulent stem of a rainforest plant. It must be very fresh and still have its leaves. You also need two jars or beakers of water, and two hues of food dye (colouring) or ink.*

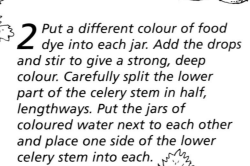

2 *Put a different colour of food dye into each jar. Add the drops and stir to give a strong, deep colour. Carefully split the lower part of the celery stem in half, lengthways. Put the jars of coloured water next to each other and place one side of the lower celery stem into each.*

2 *Carefully place the plastic bag right over the plant, and tie its open end tightly around the pot. After a short time, a 'mist' appears on the bag's inside.*

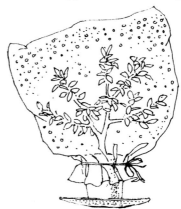

3 *Watch what happens. Invisible water vapour is given off by the leaves into the air, and liquid water is sucked up the stem to replace it. You can see the progress of the water by watching the colours move up the stem and into the leaves.*

3 *This mist comes from water vapour which has been given off by the leaves, into the air inside the bag.*
As the humidity in the bag increases, the water vapour condenses, turning back into water droplets on the plastic surface. Inside the bag, it is warm and very humid – just like a rainforest.

In the giant landmass of Asia, true rainforests occur in the south and north-east of India and in the Western Ghats. The Nicobar and Andaman islands are also covered in rainforest. India's forests have been described and catalogued by scientists in considerable detail. In addition to true rainforests, there are fifteen other major forest types, which have been divided further into 221 minor types!

India has seen extensive deforestation – from cutting down trees, from fires, and from general destruction of the forest habitat. In recent years, this deforestation has slowed. Unlike in many other parts of the world, the main reason for deforestation in India is not for wood to make furniture and other objects. It is for fuel wood, to make fires for cooking, heating and manufacturing.

With more than 750 million people in India, and numbers still rising, it is difficult to see how to halt this destruction. The situation in Bangladesh is even more serious, with more people per area of land than almost anywhere else. Only a few isolated fragments of rainforest survive, as wildlife parks, nature reserves and other protected areas.

Sunderbans
The mangrove forests in the Sunderbans of south west Bangladesh are the largest such forests in the world, with an area of 4,000 square kilometres.

Crocodiles
The estuarine or saltwater crocodile inhabits rivers, estuaries and coasts around the Indian Ocean and Australasia. It is the world's largest crocodile and has been known to kill young, inexperienced tigers. It is equally at home in the flooded areas of rainforest, among the coastal mangroves or swimming along the shoreline.

At the forest's edge

Mangrove rainforests are wet from two sources – lots of rain, and the sea. They occur mainly along estuaries and coastlines. Mangrove trees can withstand salty sea water and grow in the tidal mudflats of calm, sheltered shallow water. Their stilt-like roots hold the trees clear of the salty sea water as the tide comes in.

Tigers of the mangroves

About 350 tigers live in the Sunderbans area. This is one of the largest surviving populations of tigers in the world. The big cats love water and bathe in pools to keep cool during the heat of the day. They prey on axis (spotted) deer, wild pig or boar, water monitor lizards and smaller victims such as crabs and fish trapped in the mud or in drying pools.

Trees of Asian Rainforests

Several trees from Asian rainforests are very important as sources of timber, for furniture, decorative carvings and fine works of art. Macassar ebony has a hard black and white wood, striped like a tiger's skin. Asian types of utile look like mahogany, and were often sold as real mahogany. Rosewood has an attractive 'glow' and is used as a veneer for luxury furniture.

Other trees and plants are important for their fruits. They include the banana, durian, rambutan, mangosteen and longan. But most important by far are the mangoes, *Mangifera*.

Rosewood
One of the most valuable timbers, rosewood is purplish with darker brown or black markings.

Rattan
The tough, woody stems of this vine make 'cane' furniture, baskets and wickerwork. It is difficult to grow as a farm crop, which shows how important it is to maintain natural forests.

Banana
Not true trees, but giant herbs, bananas produce fruit – then die. Originally from South-East Asia, many varieties (cultivated kinds) are now grown worldwide.

There are 39 species of wild mangoes, most growing in tropical forests. The Indian wild mango, *Mangifera indica,* is the ancestor of the hundreds of cultivated varieties of mangoes. Some of these timber and fruit trees are grown on plantations, like farm crops. But others are still harvested mainly from the wild, since they are extremely difficult to cultivate outside the natural forest. There is also an enormous list of rainforest herbs and medicinal plants widely used by people living in the region. One book lists more than 6,000 rainforest plant species used for medicines and potions of various types.

Wild mango
Wild mangoes originally came from rainforests in India and Burma. Many varieties have been bred commercially, as have varieties of other tropical fruits.

Macassar ebony
Ebony wood is typically black. Macassar ebony also has brown markings. Like all ebonies, it is rare owing to demand for the wood.

Jungle Fliers

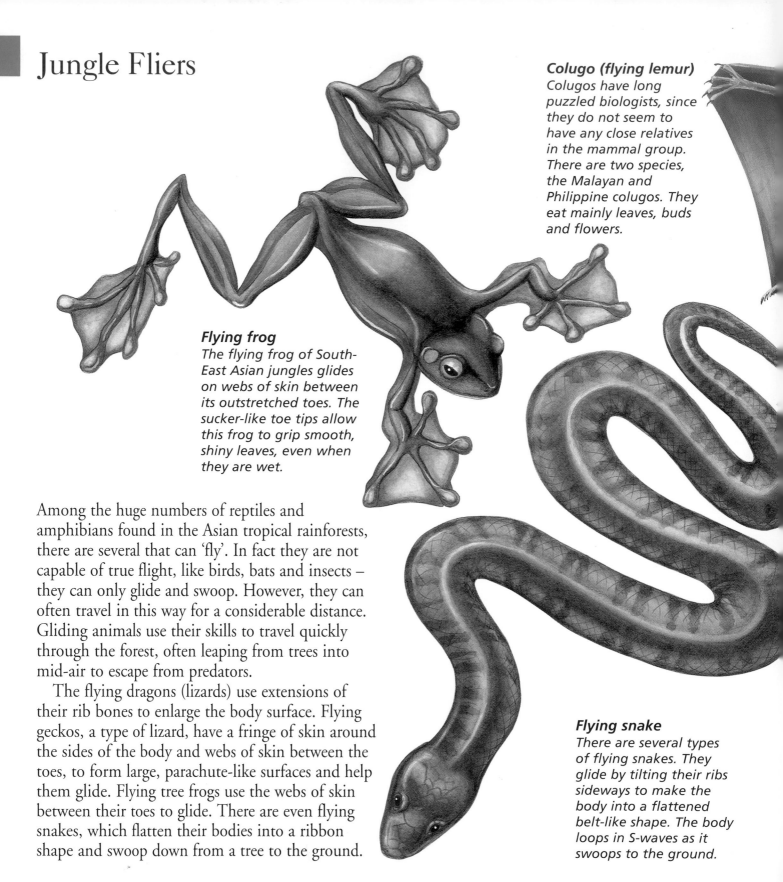

Colugo (flying lemur)
Colugos have long puzzled biologists, since they do not seem to have any close relatives in the mammal group. There are two species, the Malayan and Philippine colugos. They eat mainly leaves, buds and flowers.

Flying frog
The flying frog of South-East Asian jungles glides on webs of skin between its outstretched toes. The sucker-like toe tips allow this frog to grip smooth, shiny leaves, even when they are wet.

Among the huge numbers of reptiles and amphibians found in the Asian tropical rainforests, there are several that can 'fly'. In fact they are not capable of true flight, like birds, bats and insects – they can only glide and swoop. However, they can often travel in this way for a considerable distance. Gliding animals use their skills to travel quickly through the forest, often leaping from trees into mid-air to escape from predators.

The flying dragons (lizards) use extensions of their rib bones to enlarge the body surface. Flying geckos, a type of lizard, have a fringe of skin around the sides of the body and webs of skin between the toes, to form large, parachute-like surfaces and help them glide. Flying tree frogs use the webs of skin between their toes to glide. There are even flying snakes, which flatten their bodies into a ribbon shape and swoop down from a tree to the ground.

Flying snake
There are several types of flying snakes. They glide by tilting their ribs sideways to make the body into a flattened belt-like shape. The body loops in S-waves as it swoops to the ground.

Flying lizard
Also called the flying dragon, this lizard folds its skin flaps flat along the sides of its body when not in use. It can land on a tree trunk and grip the bark with its sharp claws.

Flying squirrel
These gliders are true squirrels that have large, thin, stretchy flaps of skin along the sides of the neck, body and tail. This flap or gliding membrane is called the patagium. The typical squirrel's bushy tail is used as a rudder for steering.

By far the best gliders are mammals. There are many species of flying squirrels in the tropical forests of Asia, but the ultimate gliders are the colugos, or flying lemurs. These are not lemurs at all, and have no particularly close relatives. One species is found only in the Philippines; another occurs from southern Indo-China to Indonesia.

When the colugo takes to the air, it glides on huge membranes which stretch between the neck and forearms, the forearms and hind limbs, and between the hind limbs and tail. One colugo flew 150 metres, yet lost only 12 metres in height.

All About Leaves

The leaves of jungle trees do many things. They catch light energy from the Sun, for the process of photosynthesis (see page 12). Their shade protects animals below from too much heat and sunshine. The leaves themselves are nutritious food for many creatures. They help to spread out and slow down raindrops, and delay their journey to the ground, so a heavy shower does not wash away the soil. And the shape of a leaf also helps us to identify the type of tree.

Leaves are also shaped to let the rainwater run off them easily. Otherwise the water might collect on them. Being heavy, the water could tear or break the leaves or their twigs and branches. Try different leaf shapes, as shown here. You need some stiff paper, flexible plastic drinking straws, sticky tape, and a water tap with a sink underneath.

1 Look around your home and garden to find interesting leaf shapes. Look especially at the leaves of houseplants that came originally from tropical forests.

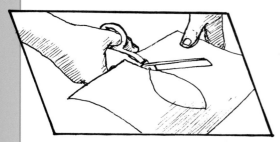 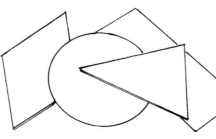 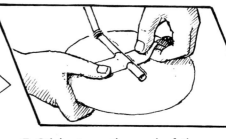

2 Carefully cut out copies of these leaves from paper. If you make all your paper leaves about the same size, the activity is slightly easier.

3 Cut out some made-up leaf shapes, too. Make these less 'natural' shapes, such as perfectly straight-sided squares, rectangles, circles and triangles.

4 Sticky-tape the end of the long section of a straw to each leaf, in the position of the leaf stalk (called the petiole). Bend up the straw's short section.

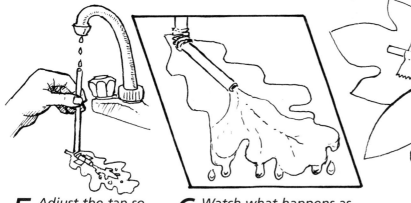

5 Adjust the tap so that it drips slowly. This is a small shower of rain in the jungle. Hold one of the leaves so its bent-up straw catches the drips.

6 Watch what happens as the drips of 'rain' run through the straw on to the leaf. Does the water flow away easily? Or does it collect and make the leaf heavy, soggy, floppy and torn?

7 Try all the paper leaves in this way. For most real leaf designs, the water is channelled by the leaf's shape. It runs away and drips off easily. Which is the best shape for shrugging off water in this way? Which is the worst shape for making water collect and damage the leaf?

Trees and Wood

The most valuable woods in the world, such as teak and mahogany, come from tropical rainforests. They are strong and long-lasting, and if they are cut or carved and polished properly, they are also very beautiful. Many lesser-known woods used for furniture, fine carvings and works of art also come from jungles and rainforests. These activities show how we depend on all kinds of woods.

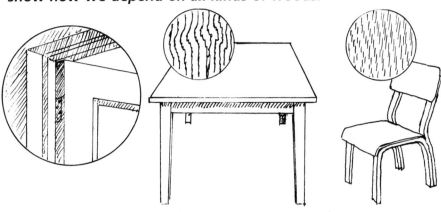

1 Look around your home for examples of woods and how they are used. The doors, door frames, window surrounds and window frames may be wood. These are usually softwoods from conifer trees such as pines, firs and spruces. They are grown in specially managed forests across northern Europe, northern Asia and North America. The wood itself is fairly soft, and the grain (direction of the small dark marks) and growth rings are easily visible.

2 See if you can find something made from a tropical hardwood such as teak or mahogany. It might be a cup, bowl, spoon or other utensil, a statue or carving, or a piece of furniture. Notice the rich colour of the wood, and how hard and heavy it is compared to a softwood. See how the grain is usually less marked, with tiny flecks rather than prominent growth rings. The exact pattern depends on the way the wood was cut from the original tree.

3 Examine a piece of 'wooden' furniture to see if it is made from solid wood. It may be covered with veneer, which is a very thin slice or layer of wood. Inside, it is probably a manufactured board such as chipboard or particleboard, with tiny pieces held together by glues and resin. Veneers make an object look good, while saving valuable woods.
On the other hand, the covering may be plastic, coloured and patterned to resemble wood!

4 Next time you visit an old building, such as a museum, library, palace or stately home, look for more kinds of wood. In the old days, before plastics, and before metals were easily available, almost all furniture and fittings were made from wood.
These may be tropical hardwoods too. The trees were cut down in the days when jungles and rainforests covered large areas, and people were less aware of the destruction done by logging.

Asian Birds and Mammals

Among the birds of Asian rainforests, pheasants are particularly diverse in the Himalayas. Many species have spectacular plumage, but by far the most dramatic are the peacocks. Although the largest variety of species occurs in the Himalayas, in the rhododendron and other mountain forests, several species also thrive in the steamy lowland rainforests. The red jungle fowl (the ancestor of domestic chickens) and the common peacock are widespread in a range of habitats, but the peacock pheasants and arguses dwell mainly in the rainforests. In the deep gloom among the huge trees, the brilliant colouring of the pittas helps these birds to identify each other. Several species have plumage that shines or glitters – known as iridescent – when a shaft of sunlight catches it.

One of the characteristics of the wildlife of Asia is that the larger mammals are adapted

Peacock
The spectacular 'tail' of the peacock is really its train, formed by feathers on the lower rear of the body. The tail feathers are short and stiff and support the train.

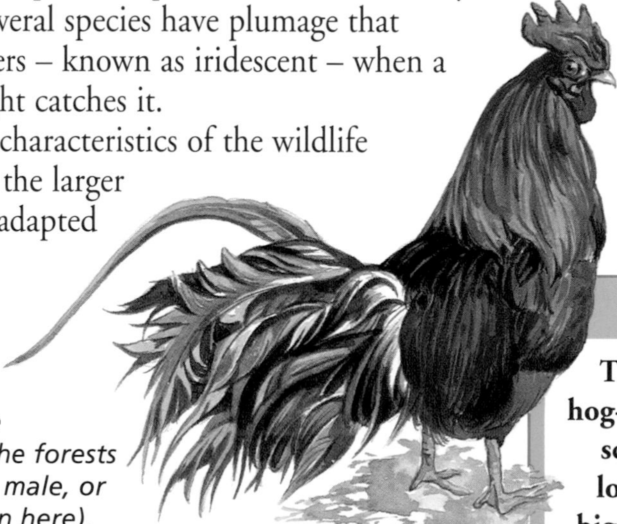

Red jungle fowl
These birds are still quite common in the forests of India. The male, or cock (shown here), usually gathers a group of four or five females, called hens.

WORLD'S SMALLEST MAMMAL

The world's smallest mammal, Kitti's hog-nosed bat, was first described by scientists in 1974. It is only 3 cm long – which is not much bigger than a large bumble bee. It lives in the moist forests of Thailand, which are very threatened by farming, water extraction and mining.

Argus
This pheasant lives deep in the forests of Malaya, Sumatra and Borneo. The male's eye-patterned train (tail) is more spectacular than the peacock's.

24

to life in forests and clearings. (In other parts of the world, such as Africa and North America, the larger mammals tend to live on the grasslands and open scrubland.) These large Asian mammals are usually solitary or live in small groups. They include axis deer, water buffalo and, of course, tigers. In the trees some monkeys and apes such as gibbons, use songs to communicate in the forest, since signalling by sight is difficult among the leaves and branches. The dawn songs of gibbons carry for more than a kilometre and let other troops of gibbons know that the local area, or territory, is occupied.

The larger mammals of Asian tropical rainforests were once widespread. But during the past century, the populations of most have plummeted towards extinction – Asian elephants and wild cattle such as the banteng, kouprey, gaur, anoa, mountain anoa and wild water buffalo. The three Asian species of rhino are even more threatened. Yet remarkably, despite unrest and conflict in the region, large mammals are still being discovered in the jungles of Indo-China.

Gibbons
These small apes can walk and even run along branches. But they move fast by brachiating – swinging through the trees with their long, muscular arms and hook-like hands.

Sambar
The large sambar deer is an important prey for tigers. Sambar were once widespread over much of Asia. As forests have been cut down, their range has split into many smaller parts.

Kouprey
In 1937 the kouprey, a giant ox, was discovered in Cambodia. In the 1990s an antelope-like species with long horns was discovered in Laos.

Rhinos
The Asian species of rhinos are the Indian, Javan and Sumatran (shown here). Extremely rare, they may not survive into the next century.

Lords of the Asian Jungle

Male
Mature males, called bulls, live on their own for part of the year. In the breeding season, they become more active and aggressive, a period called the must. They join the herd and battle each other to mate with the females, or cows.

Elephant family life
Elephants live in family groups with older females, young females and their babies, and older offspring. They move from place to place along well-worn 'elephant roads' through the dense forest.

Several species of animals from Asian forests and jungles have been domesticated for use in homes and on farms – to do work, pull goods and machines, and provide milk, meat, hides and bones.

One species that has been used by people for centuries, but which has not been truly domesticated, is the Asian elephant. It is a forest animal and smaller than its African cousin of the grasslands. It also has much smaller ears and

Matriarch
The leader of the herd is an older female called the matriarch. She may be over 50 years of age and she knows from experience where to find good food and fresh water, in each season.

relatively shorter tusks. People have a long history of catching wild elephants. They are used for ceremonial purposes, in processions and also as working animals.

Elephants are still useful in logging, as they can go into areas where motor vehicles cannot travel – and they cause far less damage to the environment. They also carry tourists in some national parks, where once they would have carried people with guns on tiger hunts.

The Jungle in Bloom

The orchids are probably the best known among the plants of the Asian tropical forests. Their brilliant colours and bizarre shapes have made them sought after by plant breeders. Unfortunately, several species have become very rare because of collecting from the wild.

The English naturalist Charles Darwin suggested the theory of evolution by natural selection partly from his observations in rainforests. He was also one of many people fascinated by orchids. In 1862 he published a book entitled *On the various ways in which British and foreign orchids are fertilised by insects*. Darwin observed that many orchids had shapes that attracted insects. He also realized that some orchid species were so specialized in shape that only a single species of insect could collect and spread the pollen.

Darwin was also fascinated by insectivorous plants, which are particularly diverse and spectacular in Asia. The pitcher plants *Nepenthes* grow so large that they can trap animals the size of shrews or frogs, as well as flies and other insects. Many pitcher plants live in trees or on very nutrient-poor soil. The animals are slowly dissolved by the plant's digestive juices, which produce nutrients that the plant can absorb to grow and stay healthy.

Orchid
The strange shapes of jungle orchids often mimic (copy) the shapes of female insects. Male insects try to mate with them, and so collect and spread the orchid's pollen.

Rafflesia
The spectacular Rafflesia *is the largest flower in the world, and also one of the most foul-smelling. The scent attracts insects which pollinate it. As recently as 1983 a new species of* Rafflesia *was discovered, with a flower nearly 1 m across and weighing 17 kg.*

Pitcher plant
The deep bowl of the pitcher contains juices to attract insects and small mammals. These tumble in and cannot climb the steep, slippery sides. They dissolve, giving the plant extra nutrients.

28

Race for the Light

All plants need light to grow. They capture its energy by the process of photosynthesis (see page 12) and use this energy for their own processes of living, making food and growing. In the rainforest, growth is so fast that young trees are in a 'race' towards any patch of light – usually a gap in the dense canopy far above. You can show how young plants respond to light using seedlings such as beans or peas. In the rainforest, all this happens much faster!

1 *You need three healthy seedlings a few centimetres tall, growing in their own pots. Put them all in the same warm, bright place, such as on a sunny windowsill. Water each one well every day during the experiment. You also need shoe boxes and black water-based paint.*

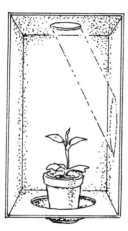

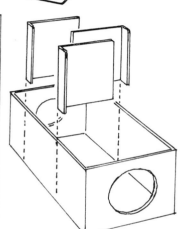

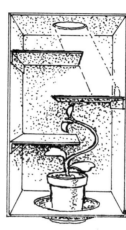

2 *One seedling will grow as though out in the open, in a forest clearing, with no nearby obstructions to shade it. There is plenty of light all around.*

3 *The second will grow in a clear patch of forest floor, towards a chink of light in the canopy above. Paint one shoe box black inside. Cut a hole in one end slightly wider than the pot, and a smaller hole in the opposite end. Put the box over the plant with the smaller hole at the top. (Water by removing the box lid.)*

4 *The third seedling will grow through a tangle of stems and vines on the forest floor, towards the canopy. Repeat step 3, but add two or three 'shelves' of card inside the box, part-way across it as shown, and also painted black. These represent the stems and leaves of other plants.*

5 *Note how the plants grow each day. With plenty of light all around, one seedling grows healthily and quite fast. The second puts lots of energy into growing tall, towards the light, but as a result, it may be paler and thinner. The third does the same and also curls around any obstacles as it grows. It is a desperate race to get ahead of other plants, and receive enough light to survive.*

29

From the Indian subcontinent, tropical forests once dominated the landscape east through Burma, and south and east through Malaya, Indonesia, the Philippines and on to Papua New Guinea and northern Australia. Today, much of that forest has gone. Some was cut down centuries ago and replaced with rice paddies and terraced hillsides. But most of the rainforest in South-East Asia has disappeared in the last fifty years. The problems in the Philippines are especially severe. Many areas are protected by laws, but there are few people to enforce them. Loggers, poachers and traders can often carry out their work at will.

In Papua New Guinea, the land is very mountainous and so of little use for farming. Huge tracts of rainforests still grow there, some of it unexplored. There are even rumours, from a national park on the island of Sumatra, of a large ape-like creature that walks upright like a human.

Bunya pine
Named from the Bunya Mountains of Queensland, Australia, the bunya pine's wood is used to make flooring, plywood and furniture. The large, sweet seeds from the cones are roasted as food.

Kauri pine
Different kinds of kauri pines grow in Malaya and Indonesia, eastern Australia, New Zealand and other Pacific islands (see also page 57). The wood has very faint, light-and-dark yearly growth rings.

Maidenhair fern
These types of ferns are widespread in many tropical forests. They have also been bred as houseplants, since they cope well with the warmth of central heating.

30

Although large animals are more noticeable, most inhabitants of the jungle are relatively small. There are thousands of different sorts of insects, snails, spiders and worms. Leeches are a problem for people and any warm-blooded animals in many rainforests. They sense the body warmth of a mammal or bird and 'loop' silently towards it, often at night, as the creature sleeps. The leech fastens its sucker-like mouth on to the skin and oozes a special juice into the wound. This contains anti-clotting chemicals so that the blood runs out freely. The leech sucks its meal, expanding like a red balloon, then loops away again. These anti-clotting chemicals, called anti-coagulants, allow the skin wound to bleed for days, bringing the risk of infection by germs in the damp forest conditions.

Cookstown orchid
This is the floral emblem of the state of Queensland. Many rainforest orchids that were once collected from the wild are now grown by plant breeders. A single perfect bloom can cost many thousands of dollars.

Australian rainforests
The tropical rainforests of Australia are mainly in the north and north-east of the continent. They are watered by moist winds blowing westwards across the Pacific Ocean. There are also temperate rainforests in the south-east and on the southern island state of Tasmania.

Fan palm
Named from its fan-shaped leaves, this palm is very tough and hardy. It can survive on thin, poor soil. Its leaves are used as porch or veranda roofing, to keep off the rain and sun.

Tree fern
These plants grow to 12 metres in height, and live mainly in the wettest rainforests. Some kinds are threatened because their trunks are shredded to make orchid compost.

Port Jackson fig
Queensland's state tree, it is rounded and spreading in shape. Figs are very important in tropical forests – their fruits are food for many animals.

31

Incredible Jungle Birds

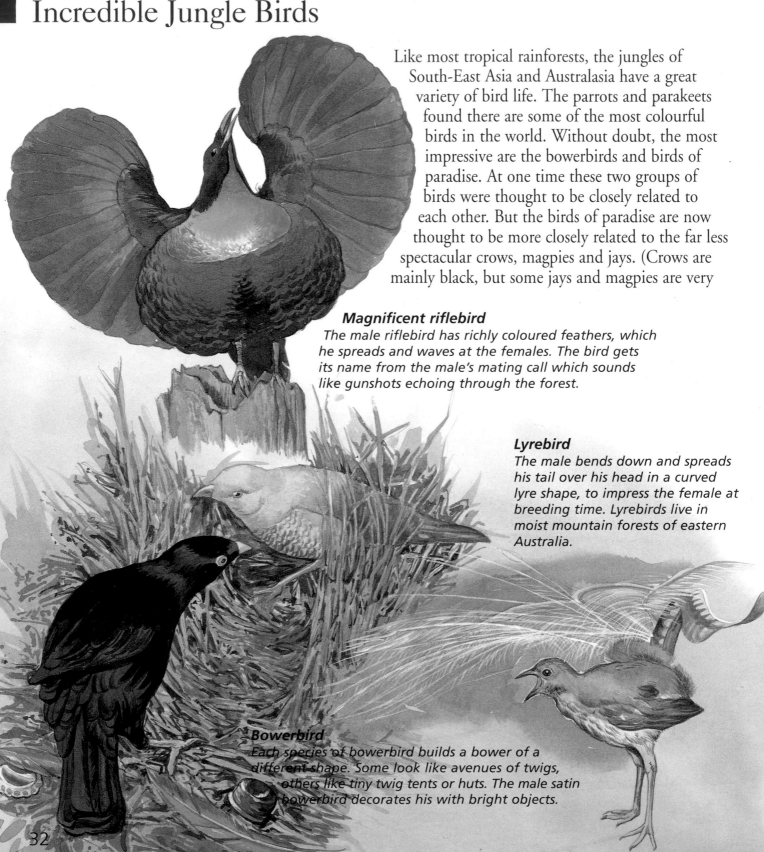

Like most tropical rainforests, the jungles of South-East Asia and Australasia have a great variety of bird life. The parrots and parakeets found there are some of the most colourful birds in the world. Without doubt, the most impressive are the bowerbirds and birds of paradise. At one time these two groups of birds were thought to be closely related to each other. But the birds of paradise are now thought to be more closely related to the far less spectacular crows, magpies and jays. (Crows are mainly black, but some jays and magpies are very

Magnificent riflebird
The male riflebird has richly coloured feathers, which he spreads and waves at the females. The bird gets its name from the male's mating call which sounds like gunshots echoing through the forest.

Lyrebird
The male bends down and spreads his tail over his head in a curved lyre shape, to impress the female at breeding time. Lyrebirds live in moist mountain forests of eastern Australia.

Bowerbird
Each species of bowerbird builds a bower of a different shape. Some look like avenues of twigs, others like tiny twig tents or huts. The male satin bowerbird decorates his with bright objects.

colourful.) Neither bowerbirds or birds of paradise are found anywhere else. The bowerbirds build bowers or 'shady, quiet playgrounds' of twigs and leaves, which some species decorate with brightly coloured objects – berries, petals and, nowadays, bits of coloured paper and plastic. The male displays at his bower to attract a mate.

The male birds of paradise rely on spectacular plumage, songs and displays to attract the females. Some of the species are found only in single valleys in the highlands of New Guinea, and their beautiful plumage may be part of the ceremonial head-dresses of the local people. About a century ago, a fashion grew up in Europe and North America for decorating hats with their feathers. Tens of thousands of the birds were killed for their plumage. Partly as a result of public outrage over killing these birds for their plumage, the first bird protection societies were set up in Europe and North America.

Eclectus parrots
Parrots are well known as cage birds, and many came originally from rainforests. They are regarded as among the most 'intelligent' of birds. They crack tough seeds and fruits with their large bills.

Cassowary and chick
The cassowary is a large flightless bird of rainforests in Indonesia, Papua New Guinea and northern Australia. Up to 1.5 metres tall, it can kick fiercely with its sharp-clawed feet.

Among the Branches

Papua New Guinea and Australia have been isolated from the rest of the world for millions of years. The mammals found there have evolved in isolation. They are mostly marsupials – pouched mammals which appeared millions of years before the main group of modern mammals, the placentals, which have a placenta (afterbirth) so the mother can feed her baby as it develops in the womb.

Marsupial mothers lack a placenta, but they have a marsupium, or pouch. The baby develops only for a short time in the womb. It is born at a very tiny, undeveloped stage and makes its way unaided to the pouch. Here it fixes on to the mother's teat to suck milk, and continues to develop. Even when the youngster is well developed, it often returns to the mother's pouch for safety.

In Papua New Guinea and Australia, various kinds of marsupials have evolved in similar ways to

Lumholtz's tree kangaroo
Also known as the boongary, this tree kangaroo is found in the mountainous rainforest of north-east Queensland. It sleeps by day curled up in the fork of a high branch.

Fawn-footed melomys
This small mammal is a rodent and so a member of the placental mammal group, not a marsupial. It lives on the forest floor in north-eastern Australia and eats fruit.

Echidna
The spiny anteater feeds on any kinds of small creatures, especially ants and termites, that adhere to its long, sticky tongue and pass into its narrow, slit-like mouth.

the placental mammals on other continents – as large grazers, small insect-eaters, gliders through the forest, underground burrowers, and so on. Among the strangest are the tree kangaroos – large browsing animals with a prehensile tail that grips the branches like a fifth limb. A new species of tree kangaroo was discovered as recently as 1990.

Even more unusual are the monotremes, or egg-laying mammals. They evolved even before the marsupials. The mother lays eggs, which hatch into tiny babies that feed on her milk. There are only three species of monotremes, and two live in

Bennett's tree kangaroo
Tree kangaroos feed on leaves and other plant material, both in the branches and on the ground. They climb into trees for safety and can leap 15 metres down to the ground.

Cuscus
The monkey-like cuscus is a marsupial, and a skilled climber in the forests of Papua New Guinea and Queensland. It eats leaves, fruits, eggs and various small creatures.

Sugar glider (gliding possum)
This small marsupial belongs to the group called ringtail possums. It licks the sweet gum or sap that oozes from cuts and breaks in the bark of trees, especially wattles and eucalypts.

tropical forests in north Australia and Papua New Guinea. They are the long-beaked and short-beaked echidnas, or spiny anteaters. They look like hedgehogs, are covered with protective spines, and they spend their lives rooting in the leaf litter, eating worms, insects and other small animals.

The 'Old Man of the Forest'

One of the largest and best-known inhabitants of
the South East Asian rainforests, yet also one of the
most shy and secretive, is the orang (orang-utan) of
Borneo and Sumatra. The name is said to mean
'Old Man of the Forest' in a local language.
Male orangs are much larger than females,
with a wider face, and they have long, coarse fur.
Forest fruits make up about two-thirds of the
orang's diet. They also eat young leaves, insects, small
animals, eggs and baby birds. They obtain extra minerals by
eating soil.

   Orangs usually live alone, except for a mother
with her youngster, who stay together for up to seven years. These
fascinating animals are protected by law, and since their main habitat
is the hot, wet, steamy rainforest, poaching is less of a
problem these days. The main threat is habitat destruction, as the
forest trees are felled for timber.

Hands and feet
*An orang seems to
have four arms – its
hips and legs are very
flexible, and its feet
can grip almost as
well as the hands.*

36

Tall Trees

How tall are the trees in your home area, compared to the huge rainforest trees that tower to 60 metres or more? You can estimate the height of a tree with the help of a friend, to make the comparison.

1 You need a friend's help, and also a tape measure, a long stick or metre rule, and a pencil. Start by measuring your friend's height with the tape measure.

2 Ask your friend to stand by the base of a tall tree. Walk about 30–50 metres away, where you have a clear view of friend and tree.

3 Hold the stick or rule out straight and upright, at arm's length. Line up its lower end with the base of the tree and your friend's feet.

4 Hold the stick steady, and with one eye closed and steady, make two marks on the stick with the pencil. These should line up with the top of your friend's head and the top of the tree.

5 Measure the pencil marks to see how many times taller the tree is than your friend. Then multiply your friend's real height by this number, to give the real height of the tree. Is it 60 metres?

Jungle trees grow very tall, but their roots do not usually penetrate very deeply, because the rainforest soil layer is relatively thin. Many of the trees have buttresses to help them stand up straight and not topple over – as you can demonstrate with these models.

1 You need plenty of stiff card, safe scissors, and sticky tape or glue. Make a model jungle tree about 30 centimetres high from stiff card, cutting out the shapes of the branches and leaves. The main trunk is a cylinder or roll of card, as wide as your finger.

2 Try balancing the tree without any roots. It is very difficult! Make a set of roots by cutting out a card disc about 10 centimetres across. Tape it to the bottom of the trunk. How easy is it to balance now? Is there a weak point between trunk and roots?

3 Add buttresses by fixing tall triangle shapes of card to the root disc and tree trunk. The buttressed tree should now be easier to balance, and it stands up more securely.

There are still large areas of untouched rainforest in Africa, especially in the centre and west of the great continent. A few are protected by law, and are some of the richest areas for wildlife on our planet. But other areas are under great threat from farming, mining, industry and human settlement.

In particular, the rainforests of the island of Madagascar, east of Africa, are both unique and endangered. Madagascar is one of the largest islands in the world, and its eastern side was once largely covered with tropical forests of various kinds.

However, during the past fifty years, this treasure-house of plant and animal life has been destroyed at an alarming rate. From 1950 to 1985, an average of 1,110 square kilometres of forest were destroyed every year. This is an annual loss which is more

Fossa
The largest predator on Madagascar, the fossa is a cat-like member of the mongoose and civet group. It hunts equally well on the ground or in rainforest trees, as it pursues lemurs, lizards, snakes and other victims.

Shrew tenrec
Like its namesake the shrew, this tenrec is active through the day and night, with short rest periods. It must eat its own weight in worms, grubs and other small creatures every day.

Ruffed lemur
Most active from dusk to midnight, this lemur feeds on leaves, fruits, berries and shoots. It hardly ever comes down to the ground.

Aye-aye
The eerie aye-aye, ghostly in appearance, taps tree bark at night with its extraordinary third finger, to find grubs beneath.

Flap-necked chameleon
The chameleon shown here has been among leaves, since it has changed its colour to green. On bark, it would become grey or brown. If threatened by an enemy such as a snake, it goes black with yellow spots, and hisses loudly!

than the entire area of the nearby island of Mauritius, once home to the now-extinct dodo.

Most of Madagascar's forest mammals (and other wildlife) are endemic – that is, they occur nowhere else in the world. The lemurs are a group of primates, relatives of monkeys and apes, that range in size from tiny mouse-lemurs to the indri, which stands about one metre tall. Perhaps the strangest of the lemurs is the aye-aye. This night-active creature feeds on insect grubs in decaying wood. It listens for their movements, gnaws away the wood with its rodent-like teeth, and extracts the grubs with a claw on its very long third finger.

The tenrecs, small insect-eaters, are also unique to Madagascar. Some resemble shrews, others have spines like hedgehogs, and others are aquatic, like water voles. Chameleons occur widely in the forests of Africa, and are especially varied in Madagascar. The largest is longer than your arm, and the smallest is shorter than your thumb.

Among African Trees

The greatest stretches of rainforest in Africa are in the centre and west, especially in countries such as Zaïre, Congo, Gabon, Cameroon, Nigeria and Côte d'Ivoire (Ivory Coast). The West African rainforests are richest and most luxuriant near the coast, especially along the east-west coastline of the Gulf of Guinea. This land receives the fullest soakings from the rain-laden monsoons sweeping in from the sea to the south and west. It is also well protected from the drying, sand-laden *harmattan* winds sweeping down from the Sahara, far to the north.

African rainforests are the original homes of many of the timber trade's most sought-after trees. Some are substitutes for teak, which came originally from South-East Asia and is still one of the world's most valued hardwood timbers. However demand far outstrips supply, so 'African teaks' are grown as replacements. They include African cordia and afrormosia, especially from the Ghana region.

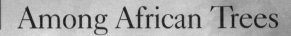

African grey parrots
These birds clamber among the branches and vines using their beaks and feet, looking for fruits, berries and nuts.

Okapi
This plant-eating forest-dweller is related to the giraffe. It dwells deep in the rainforests of Zaïre. Long hunted by local people for meat, skins and bones, it was discovered and described by scientists only in 1901. Okapis eat leaves, shoots, buds, fruits, ferns and many other types of plant food. They live alone, except for a mother and her single young, who may stay together for five years.

African linsang

A type of civet related to the fossa on page 38, the linsang is agile, nocturnal (night-active) and arboreal (tree-dwelling). It catches insects, small mammals like mice, and young birds. It may also feed on fruits and other plant parts. Its long tail helps it to balance in the branches.

Agile mangabey

Monkeys abound in the rainforests of Africa. Agile mangabeys come down to the ground more than most other kinds, to feed and drink. They eat a varied diet of insects and small animals, eggs, fruit, leaves and shoots. Sometimes they leave the forest to raid farm crops.

Iroko is a 'king tree' associated with royalty. Traditionally it was not felled by local farmers, but it is cut by commercial loggers. Lighter woods grown as beech substitutes are obeche or wawa, more than 30 metres tall with a trunk one metre in diameter. There are also West African versions of mahogany such as khaya, utile and sapele. In a few areas, the forestry methods are sustainable – that is, they cause little harm to the local environment. They also provide valuable income for local people. But in other places, the logging is uncontrolled. Vast areas of rainforest have been destroyed.

The flowers and blooms of African rainforests are as colourful as any in the world. Many familiar houseplants come from the region. One of the most common, the African violet, is now grown in millions for the plant trade, in a wide range of colours. But its wild ancestors are very rare, confined to a few mountain forests in Tanzania.

Wild African violet

The original wild African violets are now extremely threatened, because of collecting for the plant trade. Yet cultivated varieties are found in homes in almost every city around the world. These plants thrive in warmth, away from bright sunlight – just like their original rainforest home.

Our Closest Relatives

Scientific studies on evolution, fossils, body structure, body chemistry and genes suggest that our closest living relatives are the chimpanzees of West African rainforests and shrubland. In fact, our own genes are more than 98 per cent identical with those of chimpanzees.

This does not mean that we are descended from chimpanzees. It is more likely that both we and they evolved from the same ape-like ancestor, and that the human and chimpanzee ancestries split around 6–10 million years ago. Chimpanzees have always been adapted to forest life. Early humans probably came down from the trees and walked upright as the climate in their part of Africa became drier, and grasslands took over from trees.

Chimpanzees eat mainly ripe fruits from the forest trees. They also like young leaves, soft shoots and buds. They live together in loose-knit communities of 100 or more and, within these, they form party groups of five or six.

However, they are not always peaceful vegetarians. Members of a group, especially young males, may gather into a 'raiding party' and attack other creatures such as monkeys, pigs, antelopes and birds. Sometimes these victims are eaten. At other times, they are simply left to die.

Social animals
Chimpanzees communicate by a wide range of chatters, screeches and other calls, and by facial expressions and body postures. They groom each other to show 'friendship', combing the fur with their fingers, and eating any lice, fleas or other pests that they find.

Troops and territories
The make-up of a chimpanzee group is very varied. Animals may come and go from one troop to another. However some of them are not accepted by a new group. They are chased away, and they may even be caught and killed. Young chimpanzees stay with their mothers for two or even three years.

Looking down to the ground
Chimpanzees move easily among the branches of the forest canopy, searching for a tree with ripe fruit. They also eat leaves, nuts, shoots and bark, and they catch small animals such as insects and baby birds. They often come down to the ground to feed, but they flee back into the branches if threatened by an enemy such as a leopard. At night, each chimpanzee bends and weaves twigs and small boughs to make a sleeping nest.

A World in a Tree

Each tree in the rainforest is food, shelter, home and habitat to myriad animals. Larger and more mobile creatures such as birds, mammals and reptiles come and go, but some small animals may live their entire lives on one tree.

Tunnellers and burrowers, like moles and rodents, dig among the roots. Woodpeckers walk over the bark, pecking it away to get at grubs, beetles and other tasty items underneath. Snakes slither through the branches, creeping up on unwary chicks in their nest. Agile cats such as the leopard rest on a bough, or drag their kill to the fork of a branch, to eat it and store the leftovers.

Spiders spin their webs among the twigs, while the flowers and fruits swarm with ants, bees, wasps, butterflies, flies and thousands of other insects. The constant fall of leaves, quickly rotting in the moist, shady warmth below, supports a mini-jungle of worms, slugs, snails, millipedes, centipedes, beetles, ants, termites and other leaf-litter creatures.

Leopard
The most adaptable big cat, the leopard is equally at home in rainforest or semi-desert. It sleeps stretched out on a bough, in a patch of sunlight.

Red-billed hornbill
After the female lays her eggs in the tree-trunk nesting hole, the male plasters the entrance with mud. She and her offspring are walled in and protected from predators. They depend on the male to bring them food and drink.

Black-headed oriole
Orioles live in tropical forests across Africa, Asia and Australasia. They feed in trees on fruits and insects. Their beautiful, clear song can be heard over long distances at dawn and dusk.

Wasps and bees
Some kinds of bees and wasps live alone. Others build nests and live in groups. The nest may be in a hole in the tree. Or the wasps make a nest from chewed wood, which sets like cardboard.

Driver (army) ants
Ants are the 'cleaners' of the forest. They cut up and gather all kinds of substances to eat, from old leaves and fruits, to rotting animal bodies.

Growing Seeds and Nuts

Many of the fruits, vegetables and nuts that we buy from food stores were originally jungle plants. If you re-create the warm, moist conditions of the tropical rainforest, you may be able to make their seeds – the pips or nut kernels – germinate and grow. In general, you need to keep them at a temperature of at least 18°C, even at night, and prune them or they will grow too large. But don't try looking in bananas for seeds to grow. Commercial bananas have been bred to be seedless, and new plants are made from cuttings.

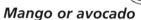

Orange or lemon

Plant several pips about a thumb's width down in damp potting mixture, in a dark and warm place. When the shoots appear, carefully put each plant in a separate pot in a bright, warm place, and water it every day or two.

Mango or avocado

Wash or clean the 'stone', which is the seed. Use 3–4 cocktail sticks stuck into the seed to hold it suspended in a jar of fresh water. Keep the jar in a warm, dim place with the water always topped up. When the roots emerge after several weeks, plant carefully in a pot of sandy compost. Put it in a warm, bright place, watering daily.

Pineapple

Carefully cut the spiky-leaved top from the whole fresh pineapple, leaving about 3 centimetres of fleshy fruit. Scoop out the flesh, leave to dry for three days, remove the lowest leaves and plant in a damp, sandy soil. Spray the whole plant with water daily.

Coffee

You need fresh, unroasted coffee beans. Plant in a pot of warm, damp potting mixture, in a dark place. As a bean sprouts, keep it in a shady place and slightly cooler, around 15–18°C. The new coppery leaves soon turn glossy green.

Ginger

Fresh ginger root may sprout if you skewer it on 2–3 cocktail sticks or a kebab stick, and suspend it mostly under water in a jar. When it sprouts roots, plant it in a pot of standard compost, keeping it warm, light and well watered.

New World Rainforests

The tropical forests of the New World once stretched almost unbroken from parts of Mexico, down through Central and South America, to the cooler zones of Argentina and Chile. But in the past fifty years they have been ravaged by clearing, logging, burning, ranching and farming, and the pressure continues.

The mahogany forests have mostly been cut down, and huge areas of countries like Costa Rica and Brazil have been cleared of their forests to make way for cattle pasture. One of the main reasons for the clearances was to raise cows and sell the beef for the worldwide hamburger market!

Some countries have now introduced controls on logging. The price of timber continues to rise, so it is possible to make profits by 'managing' the forest – cutting down some trees while leaving others.

Layers of the forest
Looking from the side, the forest has natural layers or levels, often called storeys. They range from the tallest emergent trees, their topmost branches in bright sunshine, to soil far below.

Rich jungle to bare soil
As parts of the rainforest are cut down, the soil is left without plant roots to hold it in place. The soil is washed away by the heavy rains, clogging rivers and choking their wildlife.

Ground layer
Few plants grow on the ground, since there is little light under the dense canopy. Some ferns can put up with the gloomy conditions. Fungi abound, rotting wood and leaves in the humid warmth.

Soil
Rainforest soil is surprisingly thin and poor. This is because the conditions for life are so good that nutrients are soon taken up by shrubs and trees.

Emergents
Here and there, the highest trees poke above the canopy. They are used as look-out perches by eagles and other hunting birds.
Monkeys sit in them to call across the forest, warning their neighbours not to trespass into their territory.

In addition to timber, the New World rainforests have many other natural products, such as rubber and chicle, as shown on the next page. Apart from these human-required materials, the forests have incredibly beautiful and diverse wildlife. Nowhere on Earth are so many kinds of trees, flowers, herbs, insects, birds and other life forms packed together into such small areas, living together in such complicated ways.

One of the most interesting groups of American plants are the figs. Wild figs are an extremely important part of forest life, because their abundant and nourishing fruit is eagerly sought by many of the forest animals (see page 31), including monkeys, bats and birds. The different kinds of fig trees fruit at different times of the year, so the animals move through the forest in search of trees with ripening fruit. In so doing, they carry the fig seeds far and wide, spreading the trees.

Canopy
Like a dense green blanket many metres above the ground, the canopy is a tangled mass of small branches, twigs, leaves, shoots, buds, flowers, fruits and abundant animal life (see page 50).

STRANGLED TO DEATH

The strangler fig starts life as a vine around a forest tree (1). As it grows, it gradually engulfs the tree – and kills it (2). The wood rots and the strangler continues to thrive (3). It becomes a huge, hollow 'tree', home for a range of wildlife, including bats, coatis, potoos, even jaguars.

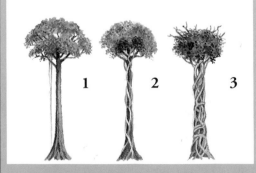

Shrub layer
Under the canopy, various plants struggle to grow in the dimness. They include young trees, shrubs, creepers and tall herbs. When a large tree dies and falls, leaving a gap in the canopy, light shines through and encourages their growth.

Plant Life of the Amazon

The rainforests of Central and South America have provided innumerable useful products in addition to dozens of kinds of wood. They include fruits and other foods, flavourings, medicinal drugs, dyes and pigments (colouring substances), natural chemicals and flowers. There are drugs such as quinine against the disease malaria. Vanilla, a flavouring common in ice cream, comes from orchids that grow wild in Central and South America.

A surprising number of plants grown in our homes and gardens come from tropical American

Curare
The native peoples in the forests of South America used a poison known to Europeans as curare or wourali, obtained from the roots of a vine or tree growing in the forest. From this poison, scientists developed a drug used in medicine to relax muscles.

Quinine
The Indians of Ecuador and Peru used an extract from the cinchona tree to make quinine, an important medicine that relieves fever. The Dutch and British later took it to Asia, and in India it became an important ingredient in tonic water.

forests. Morning glories range in colour from sky blue to red and purple, and the sweet potato is in fact a species of morning glory. Cannas grow wild along the edges of forests. Trees often have bromeliads growing on them. These are generally greyish-leaved plants, and some varieties are also known as 'air plants' since they seemingly thrive on fresh air, without soil. Perhaps the best known of these natural bounties is the pineapple. The first European to taste one may have been Christopher Columbus in 1493. Although pineapples are now grown in areas that were once covered with tropical

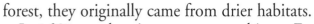

forest, they originally came from drier habitats.

In 1657 an advertisement appeared in an English newspaper for a drink called chocolate, made from the cocoa fruit. The trees from which the cocoa pods came grew in the tropical forests of Peru and other parts of Central and South America. Most of these plants are now cultivated, but some are still gathered from the wild. One is allspice, collected in tiny quantities from the forests of Belize.

Air plants
Some bromeliads are popular as 'air plants'. In nature, they absorb water and nutrients from rain running down the tree, so they need very little soil. A common type is Spanish moss, which hangs down like thick, tangled cobwebs.

Cocoa (chocolate)
Originally flavoured with hot peppers by the Mexicans, chocolate was always a drink. In the nineteenth century, Europeans devised ways of turning it into the eating chocolate so popular today.

Vanilla
The name of this flavouring comes from the Spanish word vaina meaning a 'small pod' – the orchid's pod from which vanilla is extracted. Several species of vanilla orchids grow as climbers on trees in the humid American forests.

Nasturtiums
These popular garden plants have been cultivated to produce a range of colours, from oranges and reds to yellows, and also double-flowered varieties. Their wild ancestors grew in the moist forests of southern Mexico down to Chile.

49

Riot in the Canopy

Eagle
Many birds of prey fly over the forest canopy, watching for victims such as monkeys, opossums, sloths, coatis and other birds. The harpy eagle of Amazonia is the world's largest eagle.

Oriole blackbird
Remarkably similar to the golden oriole of the Old World, this adaptable South American bird lives in forests and also on grasslands. It has adapted to life in parks and gardens.

Three-toed sloth
One of five sloth species in New World forests, this sloth hangs by hook-like claws and eats leaves and soft buds. It has poor eyesight but a keen nose.

Moths
By day, moths rest in cracks or crevices, or among foliage. If disturbed, they reveal their large 'eyespots'.

Common iguana
This lizard climbs well with its sharp-clawed feet and long, balancing tail. It prefers trees near water, and eats all kinds of plant matter. There are more than 600 iguana species, nearly all from the New World.

Until recently, little was known about life high in the rainforest canopy. Only when large trees were felled or brought down in a storm was it possible to look at the plants and other wildlife of the tree tops. However, scientists have recently found ways of observing life in the canopy. 'Tramways' through the branches allow people to walk among the leaves and see the wildlife at close range.

High in the trees, you see a totally different view. In contrast to the quiet, still gloom of the forest floor, the canopy is packed with colour, action and sounds. Birds such as hummingbirds feed on the

Cock-of-the-rock
The brilliant red crest and back of the male are among the brightest of all animal colours. These birds live in the steep forests along river gorges in the Andes Mountains.

Scarlet macaw
One of the best-known parrots, the scarlet macaw is popular with photographers, painters and cage-bird breeders. It has become rare in some areas owing to destruction of its rainforest home.

Butterflies
These bright insects flit through the canopy and sip nectar from flowers. Their hues attract mates, and in some species they are warning colours to predators: 'Don't touch me, I taste horrible!'

Emerald tree boa
This boa lies perfectly still, looking like a bunch of leaves or a green vine – until it suddenly reaches out to grab a bird, bat or other creature with its strong front teeth.

blossoms, and monkeys eat the fruits. At night, bats and moths emerge. The range of life is truly astonishing. Some tropical rainforests have more than 100 species of trees in each hectare, many times the number found in a typical European or North American forest.

This diversity of trees is reflected in the other plants and in the animals – especially insects. There are thousands of insect species in one single hectare. Some are found only on one particular kind of tree.

Toco toucan
All thirty-seven toucan species live in South American rainforests. The toco toucan, one of the largest, has learned to feed in sugarcane and coconut plantations. It even comes into houses for food, and to tease pets!

Rainforest Monkeys

Squirrel monkey
Like many South American monkeys, the squirrel monkey has taken to raiding the crops grown on land which was once rainforest. It lives in bands or troops of 20, 30 or even more.

Monkeys are characteristic mammals of the forest canopy throughout tropical rainforests. They are often rather messy feeders, allowing part-eaten fruits such as figs, as well as blossoms and leaves, to fall to the ground. Luckily this provides food for animals below that are unable to climb, such as tapirs, peccaries and agoutis. New World monkeys have evolved separately from their Old World cousins. Some have a prehensile tail that can grip the branches like a fifth limb, and their whoops and calls echo across the green canopy.

Emperor tamarin
One of fifteen tamarin species, the emperor tamarin dwells in the north-western Amazon region. It is very active, constantly searching for food, from leaves to grubs.

Pygmy marmoset
Small enough to sit on your hand, this tiny monkey stays still for many seconds, then dashes through the leaves and branches. It moves like this to avoid predators, especially birds.

Spider monkey
There are several types of spider monkeys, and all are amazingly agile in the tree tops. They feed mainly on fruit and move in noisy, active groups, chiefly in early morning and late afternoon.

White-fronted capuchin
Like many New World monkeys, the active and inquisitive white-fronted capuchin can grip branches with its curly prehensile tail.

The monkey's main competitors when feeding in the forest canopy are birds. In temperate regions, birds usually form flocks of one species. In the tropics, mixed flocks are common. They number a hundred birds or more, but with only a few individuals of each species in the flock.

Black howler monkey
Almost as large as a chimp, the black howler is named from its ear-splitting shouts, howls and whoops, as it signals to others of its kind. Only males are black; females are brown.

LION TAMARINS IN PERIL

The tamarins are small, squirrel-like monkeys from southern Central America and Amazonia. The golden lion tamarins are extremely threatened, with numbers only in the hundreds. They survive in just a few tiny areas in Brazil, near Rio de Janeiro and São Paulo, and in Bahia.

Lion tamarins are protected by law, but some are still captured for the illegal pet trade, and even for people to eat. Nature reserves of undisturbed tropical rainforest have been set up to save these highly endangered creatures. They eat flowers and fruits, and lap at plant saps, gums and nectar. They also prey on small creatures such as insects, snails, lizards and frogs.

Douroucouli
This creature is also called the night monkey, since it is one of only a few medium-sized monkeys active during darkness. Its varied diet ranges from leaves and fruits to birds' eggs, insects and spiders.

The Blood-lapping Vampires

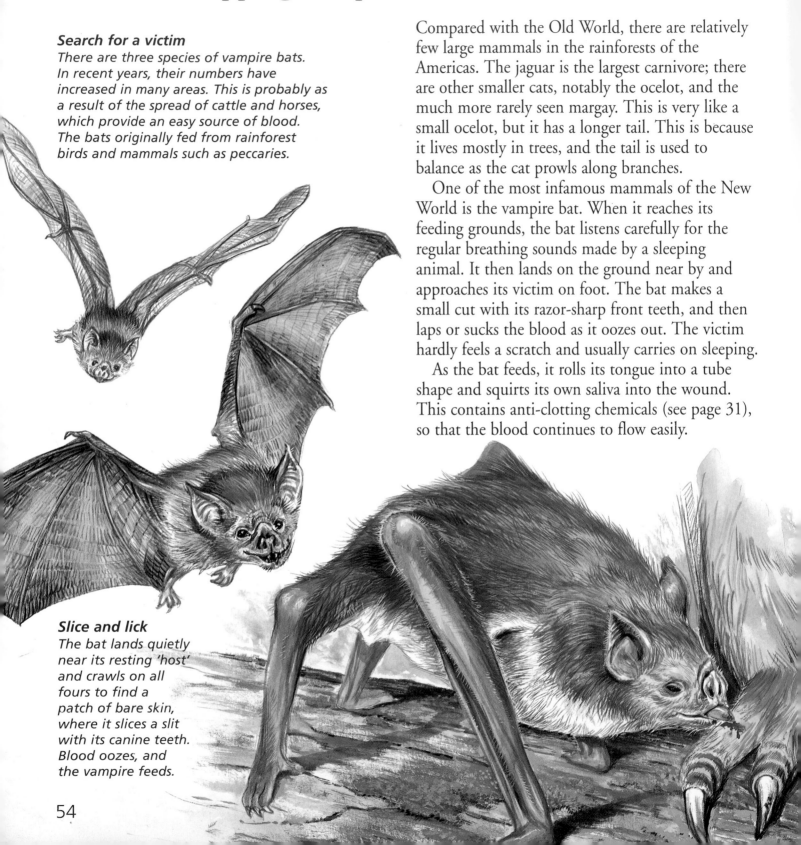

Search for a victim
There are three species of vampire bats. In recent years, their numbers have increased in many areas. This is probably as a result of the spread of cattle and horses, which provide an easy source of blood. The bats originally fed from rainforest birds and mammals such as peccaries.

Compared with the Old World, there are relatively few large mammals in the rainforests of the Americas. The jaguar is the largest carnivore; there are other smaller cats, notably the ocelot, and the much more rarely seen margay. This is very like a small ocelot, but it has a longer tail. This is because it lives mostly in trees, and the tail is used to balance as the cat prowls along branches.

One of the most infamous mammals of the New World is the vampire bat. When it reaches its feeding grounds, the bat listens carefully for the regular breathing sounds made by a sleeping animal. It then lands on the ground near by and approaches its victim on foot. The bat makes a small cut with its razor-sharp front teeth, and then laps or sucks the blood as it oozes out. The victim hardly feels a scratch and usually carries on sleeping.

As the bat feeds, it rolls its tongue into a tube shape and squirts its own saliva into the wound. This contains anti-clotting chemicals (see page 31), so that the blood continues to flow easily.

Slice and lick
The bat lands quietly near its resting 'host' and crawls on all fours to find a patch of bare skin, where it slices a slit with its canine teeth. Blood oozes, and the vampire feeds.

Caring for Jungles and Rainforests

Many plants for the house, greenhouse and garden came from tropical forests. So do various kinds of wood, and also many foods, especially fruits and vegetables, and even animals in petshops, wildlife parks and zoos. With the help of books or CD-roms from your school and local library, try to find out how much we rely on rainforests for many of the materials, plants, produce and animals around us.

You can help to care for jungles and rainforests in many ways, such as by asking if the products from them were produced in a sustainable (long-term use), environmentally careful way. You could join a campaign group (see page 70).

1 Visit a timber merchant and find out which hardwoods are stocked. See if you can find out where they come from, by asking questions or reading leaflets.

1 Check information leaflets, price labels and the words on containers and packages. Do they mention environmentally careful, ecologically friendly and sustainable (long-term use) methods?

2 Visit a supermarket and see how many fruits, vegetables, seeds, nuts and other foods came from tropical forests. There is often information on the price labels or packages.

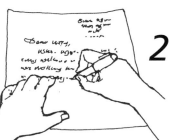

2 Write to the main office of local supermarkets. Ask if they have a policy to buy their hardwoods, fruits or other products in a way that does not damage or destroy the environment.

3 Visit a wildlife park or zoo and see how many animals you can find that originally came from tropical forests. Would the park or zoo be as exciting without them?

3 Ask campaigning and environmental groups if they have leaflets, posters and other information about saving jungles and rainforests.

4 Visit a botanical garden, especially the greenhouses and hothouses, and see how many plants there are from the rainforests. Ask the staff for information about tropical forests.

4 Suggest to your school, club or other group that you could do projects and topics on jungles and rainforests. You could find out more about them and how to save them.

Japanese red cedar
Individual matchstick-sized leaves on this tree live for about five years. But each autumn they fill with natural 'anti-freeze' chemicals to protect them against the cold and frosts of winter. The chemicals are red, hence the tree's common name.

The most threatened of all the world's rainforests and moist forests are the temperate rainforests of cooler lands. This is because there are very few of them, they are relatively small in area, and they are easily logged. The largest areas of temperate rainforests occur in the Australian island of Tasmania, in Washington State in the USA, near the southern tip of South America, in New Zealand's South Island, and in Japan.

Yakushima is one of Japan's smallest islands. It contains a fragment of the temperate rainforest that once covered much of the other islands. This island was still being logged until the 1960s, and only one-fifth of the original forest now remains, but it contains cedars over 3,000 years old. One, called the Jomon Sugi

Swamp cypress
From the wet areas of south-eastern North America, the swamp cypress can withstand having its roots submerged and waterlogged for long periods. Its timber resists rot and decay.

Redwood
Redwoods thrive in the narrow strips of moist forest along the 'fog belt' coast of north-western North America. Some trees are over 100 metres tall and their bark is thick, soft and stringy.

cedar, may be 7,200 years of age. The forest is dense with undergrowth – ferns, mosses, liverworts and fungi cover fallen branches and tree stumps.

Similarly, the moist, cool forests of Washington State and eastern North America contain huge redwoods and Douglas firs. At the other end of the Americas are the Valdivian forests stretching along the coast of southern Chile. Here the southern beech trees are overgrown with ferns, mosses and other epiphytes (plants that grow on trees). The dense, wet, cool undergrowth forms a virtually impenetrable, ever-dripping thicket.

Chilean beech (Raoul)
From the Andes Mountains, this beech is planted in many other countries, for its fast growth and fine wood.

Kauri pine
Various species of kauris thrive in cooler moist forests (see also page 30). Some have broad leaves rather than thin needles.

TEMPERATE FOREST DWELLERS

Compared to the riot of life, colour and noise in a tropical rainforest canopy, temperate rainforests have fewer animals. However, there are still many fascinating and famous creatures living there, including birds, deer, bears and predators from the dog and cat family. Tasmanian forests have a selection of marsupials that look like the cats and shrews from other continents.

Mule deer
Also called the black-tailed deer, and now rare in many places, this animal wanders the forests of western North America and also Central America.

Spectacled bear
The only bear in South America, this creature lives in moist forests and also among the mountain crags of the northern Andes.

Quoll
Known as the native cat, the quoll is a fierce hunting marsupial of forests in eastern Australia.

Kiwi
Sniffing with the nostrils at the tip of its long beak, this New Zealand flightless bird feeds on forest-floor foods.

A Double Life

In the north-west of North America, close to the border between Canada and the USA, is an area of temperate rainforest. Often covered with mists and rainclouds, these forests are home to many animals found nowhere else in the world. Because of the high humidity, at least seventeen species of amphibians are found in this region, including one of the largest known salamanders – the Pacific giant salamander, which can grow to 35 centimetres long.

The climbing salamanders are very agile and have been found more than six metres up in trees. They often lay their eggs (spawn) in a mass of jelly under tree bark, or in holes in rotten logs, where they are less likely to dry out. The yellow-blotched

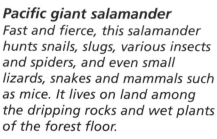

Pacific giant salamander
Fast and fierce, this salamander hunts snails, slugs, various insects and spiders, and even small lizards, snakes and mammals such as mice. It lives on land among the dripping rocks and wet plants of the forest floor.

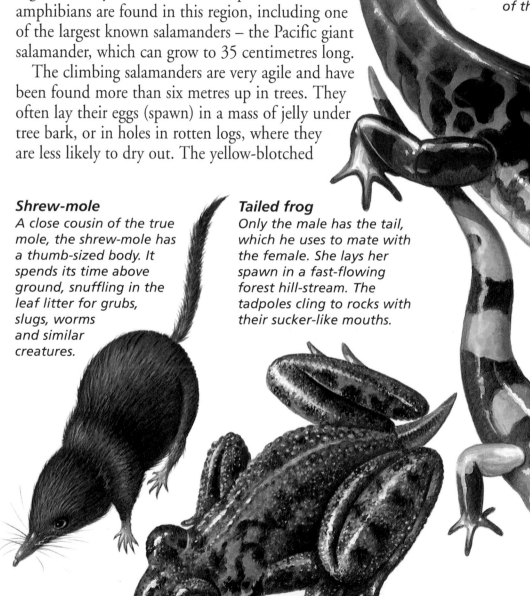

Shrew-mole
A close cousin of the true mole, the shrew-mole has a thumb-sized body. It spends its time above ground, snuffling in the leaf litter for grubs, slugs, worms and similar creatures.

Tailed frog
Only the male has the tail, which he uses to mate with the female. She lays her spawn in a fast-flowing forest hill-stream. The tadpoles cling to rocks with their sucker-like mouths.

salamander can shed its tail when this is grabbed by a predator, in the same way as many lizards. Living in the cool, clear mountain streams is the tailed frog. As its name suggests, it has a short tail. Its only relatives live in similar temperate rainforests in New Zealand, across the vast Pacific Ocean.

There are also unique mammals, such as the shrew-mole which fits in looks and behaviour between shrews and moles. It lives in the damp floor of the forest, where it feeds on worms and other small invertebrates. The rare spotted owl also occurs in these North American forests. It has become a symbol of the controversy over whether loggers should be allowed to cut down the forests where these fascinating creatures live – with the possible loss of unique wildlife from our world.

Spotted owl

The northern variety of this owl species has become famous in the battle between US conservationists and the timber trade because timber merchants deal in the trees that form its habitat. The owl eats mainly flying squirrels and wood rats, as well as moles, squirrels, and jays and other birds.

Yellow-blotched salamander

About 15 cm long, this is one variety of the ensatina salamander, which is very variable in colour and pattern. It eats large insects such as beetles and crickets, and also spiders and slugs.

POISONOUS FROGS

Many frogs and toads make toxins, or poisons, in tiny glands in their skin. This oozes out when the creature is threatened or grabbed by a predator. The predator remembers the bright warning colours of the amphibian, and does not try to catch the same prey again. This method of defence is used by many rainforest frogs in both temperate and tropical areas.

Perhaps the best known of these are the arrow-poison frogs from Central and South America. Local peoples tipped their hunting arrows with poison from the frogs' skin, to paralyze and kill the victims they hunted, such as monkeys, tapirs and peccaries.

Fliers and Gliders

Squirrels, colugos, possums, lizards and snakes are just some of the animals who can swoop and glide through the jungle. Gliding is common in forests because there are so many trees to leap from, compared to a grassland or desert. It can be used to escape from an enemy or to travel fast in search of food or a nest. The colugo is expert at gliding from the high branch of one tree, to land on the low trunk of another tree, race up the bark using its sharp claws to a high branch, and then glide again.

You can test the shapes of gliding creatures using good-quality paper and safety scissors, as shown here.

1 An A4 piece of paper is about the right size. Fold it on one long side into a strip about the width of your finger.

2 Do this several times so that the paper is about half of its original width. Press the folds hard and flat.

3 Fold the sheet in half with the first set of folds outside. Cut out a scoop shape carefully as shown.

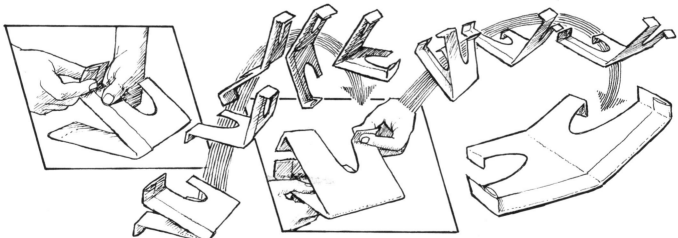

4 Score and fold the edges of the longer set of flaps, bending each finger-width strip outwards.

5 Unfold the main sheet and fold it again the other way. Score and fold another set of finger-width strips on the edges of the shorter flaps.

6 Open out the jungle glider so it is almost flat. The wide end is the front and its main wing-edge strips point up. The narrow end is the tail and its small wing-edge strips point down.

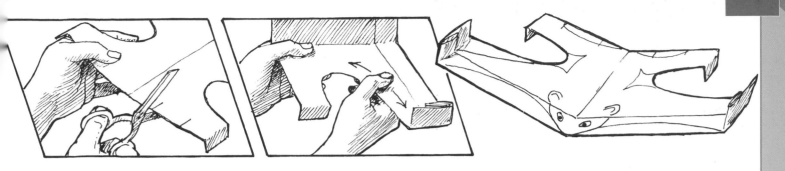

7 Make tail elevators by cutting two small snips on either side of the rear of the small tail wing, as shown. These will be adjusted to make the glider fly well.

8 Run your thumb along the rear of each main wing to make it curve and bend down slightly. This is called cambering, and it gives a parachute-like shape, like a real gliding creature.

9 Look at the 'flying' creatures on page 20. Which one does your jungle glider resemble most? Colour it with felt-tip pens to look like the real animal. You are now ready for the launch.

10 Hold the glider with your first finger at the back on top, along the midline fold, and your thumb and other fingers underneath. Move your hand forwards smoothly – and let go. Do not throw or jerk the glider. Practice different speeds of launch until it swoops through the air, like the real thing!

If it dives:
Fold the tail elevators up slightly.

If it stalls (climbs steeply, then dives):
Fold the tail elevators down slightly.

If it spins to the left:
Fold the rear corners of the main wing strips to the right.

If it spins to the right:
Fold the rear corners of the main wing strips to the left.

61

Jungles in Danger

Felling

Within minutes, one logger with a chain-saw can cut down or fell a giant rainforest tree which has lived for a hundred years. Even the small, young trees may be cut down before their prime, for quicker profits.

Despite years of concerns and campaigns, jungles and rainforests are still being destroyed at an alarming rate. Each year some 15,000 square kilometres disappear – an area half the size of Belgium. Forests are destroyed for a variety of reasons, including logging for timber, woodchip, veneers and other timber products, and to create agricultural lands or pasture. But much of this clearance is for short-term financial gain.

The people living in and around the forests rarely benefit from their destruction. They may have been using the forests in a more sustainable way to gather fuel, and to collect fruits, foods, medicines and other products. Huge profits are made by traders,

Stripping

The smaller branches may be cut off the main trunk and burned on the spot. Sometimes they are shredded by giant machines, for compost or to make various kinds of woodchip products.

Forest fires

Unwanted stumps, branches and other objects are bulldozed into a pile and burned. If an area of forest has no useful large trees, only shrubs and saplings, it is simply torched. Animals either flee or burn alive in the flames.

business people, agents and, in some cases, civil servants and politicians who grant the permits for this wholesale destruction.

Another major threat, especially in Africa, is too many people. They need wood for fuel and land for crops and farm animals. Unfortunately, when the forest is cleared, it leaves thin soil that is totally unsuited for farming. Other serious problems include reduced water supplies, conflicts and wars.

In the central African country of Rwanda, a National Park was established in 1925. In the 1980s, villagers living near the park noticed that, for the first time, their local water supply dried up. This was because forest around the park had been cleared for agriculture. One local community was so concerned that the villagers left one of the areas of land set aside for agriculture, and gave it back to the park. Much of this Rwandan rainforest had been cleared to grow pyrethrum to make insecticides – a project funded by the by the industrial West.

We must all share some blame for the loss of these marvellous habitats.

Short-term gain

In a few years, the cattle have gone and the land is bare. Thousands of rainforest plants and animals, living together in the most intricate and wonderful ways, have been destroyed – to make get-rich-quick dollars, and leave a barren wilderness.

Soil erosion

Without plants to absorb the rainwater, and tree roots to hold the soil in place, the soil washes away down the hill. It blocks rivers or makes them flood over the land, creating havoc.

Transport

The huge logs are very heavy. Transporters squash and crush the thin soil, killing its creatures and preventing air and water seeping down into it. The soil becomes compressed and dead.

Poor land

The thin, squashed soil is poor in nutrients. It may support a year or two of crops, then a few more years as cattle pasture. But soon it has lost all its goodness and turns into a rain-soaked 'desert'.

63

Saving the Rainforests

Jungles and rainforests can produce timber, raw materials and other substances in a long-term and sustainable way, if they are managed properly. Three centuries ago in the small Central American country of Belize, the loggers (who were often pirates as well) started cutting logwood, an important source of natural dyes. When artificial dyes were invented, the loggers turned to cedar, which was used for making cigar boxes and other lightweight, airtight boxes. In the present century mahogany has been cut, followed by rosewood, ziricote, cabbagewood and santa maria.

This type of limited logging – only certain tree species, on a small scale, in only some places and for short periods of time – may not do great harm.

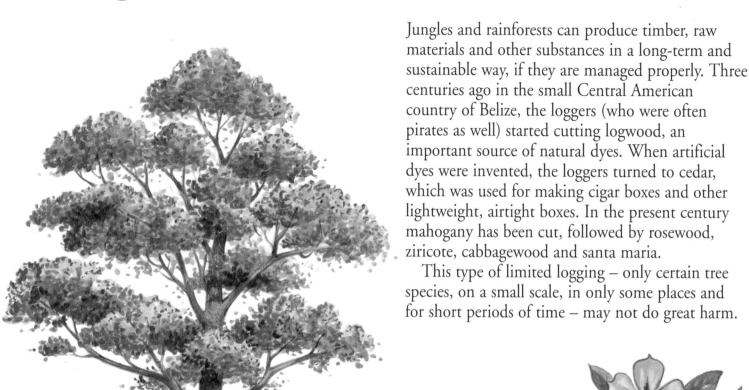

Total destruction
Clear felling destroys large areas of forest completely. There are no plants left to produce seeds, so these cannot grow again, to regenerate the forest. The area remains barren for tens or hundreds of years.

Selected logging
True mahogany is one of the most valuable woods in the world. It has a beautiful appearance and is very hard. Mahogany trees grow in the forests of tropical South America. They are about 30 metres tall, with leaves up to 30 centimetres long. If these trees are cut down only here and there, a few at a time, then damage to the habitat is limited. The forest can 'repair' itself.

Medicinal plants
The rainforests are home to thousands of herbs and other plants that may be useful for producing medicines. The rosy periwinkle from Madagascar has been used to make anti-cancer medicinal drugs. Yet hundreds of these plant species are destroyed even before they are identified.

Although most tropical forests are long-lived and relatively stable habitats, some are adapted to sudden damage, and this may help them to recover from short-term damage done by humans.

In many parts of the tropics, violent storms such as hurricanes and typhoons occur at regular intervals. The forests are adapted to cope with limited devastation, as trees are uprooted and flash floods wash away soil. Seedlings such as mahogany are able to take advantage of the clearings in the forest. In normal conditions, they would not survive in the gloom of the closed canopy of a mature forest. They grow very rapidly, and gradually, over the years, the forest grows again.

ECO-TOURISM

Before the outbreak of war in Rwanda in 1993, tourists could visit the extremely rare mountain gorillas in their high-rainforest home. The gorillas received close attention, and visitors paid large amounts of money for this ultimate wildlife experience. So the gorillas could be closely guarded and protected against poachers.

This is an example of eco-tourism. People can experience the wildlife of an area without too much harm to the habitat, and with gain to the local economy. However, war overtook the region. The future of the gorillas is once again in doubt.

Raw materials
Natural rubber is made from the milky latex or sap of rubber trees. These grow naturally in the rainforests of South America. Seeds were taken to Europe and then to Asia, where huge areas of natural rainforest were cleared to make rubber plantations.

Tapping the rubber trees
To obtain the latex, cuts are make in the rubber tree's bark. The sap oozes out and drips into collecting bowls. When the motor car was invented, huge areas of rubber trees were planted in Asia to provide rubber for their tyres.

Mining and Minerals

In general, tropical rainforest areas are not rich in the minerals valued by our modern world for industrial processes and goods. But there are some places where gold rushes happen, and open-cast mines for coal, iron, zinc and other metals scar the landscape. In the Amazon region, rumours of gold in the 1970s caused a mass rush to the upper reaches of the river. Prospectors used mercury-containing chemicals to pan and wash the riverbed deposits for gold. The toxic mercury got into the water system and poisoned millions of creatures. It made people ill and killed some, and destroyed fisheries further downstream.

Big companies can make huge profits from rainforests because the people there are often poorly educated in the ways of the modern world. But the wealth is temporary, and it kills the richest and most beautiful wildlife habitats on our planet.

Roads in the jungle
Modern machinery can build roads through a rainforest in a few weeks. This allows people to gain access more easily and begins the destruction.

Forest peoples (bottom)
In the huge African country of Zaire, forest pygmies still hunt wild animals and gather fruit and other plant food. They live in simple shelters made from branches covered with leaves.

Survival in Jungles and Rainforests

The heat, dampness and humidity in tropical rainforests mean that many people who are not used to the conditions soon feel uncomfortable, tired, hot and weak. There is also a variety of animal dangers, such as disease-carrying biting flies, blood-sucking leeches and ticks, and poisonous snakes. However, you can minimize these risks with sensible precautions. Then you can enjoy your visit to a jungle as one of the most thrilling experiences of a lifetime.

Make preparations

If you visit a tropical area, ensure that you get medical advice several months beforehand. Ask about vaccinations and other injections you might require, and about tablets and medicines to take with you or obtain when you arrive.

Never go alone

Always travel in a group, preferably at least four people. One member of the group should know the area and be familiar with jungle survival techniques and basic first aid. If you get lost or one person is injured, another can stay while the others get help.

Plan and tell others

Do not make your trip too ambitious. Pushing and cutting your way through undergrowth may look exciting in the movies, but in real life it is extremely tiring and slow. Leave information with the local ranger or guide centre about where you are going and when you should return.

Clothing

Wear strong walking boots and trousers to protect against stinging plants and possible snake bites. A long-sleeved shirt also protects against scratches. Remember that, in a rainforest, it's likely to rain! Tight or denim clothing soon soaks up moisture, and chafes and rubs the skin.

Equipment

Carry standard equipment including extra clothing, a first aid kit, knife, small hand-axe or machete, compass, large-scale maps, whistle, torch, food rations and water-sterilizing tablets. Use an approved backpack that leaves both arms free.

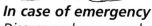

In case of emergency

Discuss and agree a plan of action. The most able and experienced group members should go for help. If you are lost, try to find a clearing. Spread out garments, a tent or sheet, or arrange rocks and branches in a pattern, visible from the air.

Leeches

Ensure that the leech lets go rather than trying to pull it off. Put salt, sugar or similar grains on to it. Or hold a flame near by to make the leech hot.

Amazing Facts

Jungles and rainforests cover less than 6 per cent of the Earth's land surface, about 9 million square kilometres.

Yet at least three-quarters of all the world's plant and animal species live in jungles and rainforests. No one knows the total number of species, but it is estimated that five out of six species of animals and plants in rainforests, are still unknown to science.

In the past 30 years, estimates of the total number of animal and plant species in jungles and rainforests have risen from half a million to more than 20 million. Many are insects.

With the current rate of destruction of rainforests and jungles, this would mean at least one undiscovered species is disappearing and being made extinct, every day.

Rainforests grow in areas where rainfall exceeds 1,800 millimetres per year. Evergreen rainforests receive up to 4,000 millimetres of rain almost constantly through the year.

Moist forests receive about 2,000 millimetres of rain yearly. Deciduous forests receive 1,500 millimetres, which falls mainly in the six-month wet season. (London's annual rainfall is 593 millimetres, and New York's is 1,100 millimetres.)

Half the world's wood grows in tropical rainforests.

Rainforests are being destroyed at an average rate of about 5 per cent each year. This is roughly equivalent to an area the size of England being lost yearly, and not being replaced.

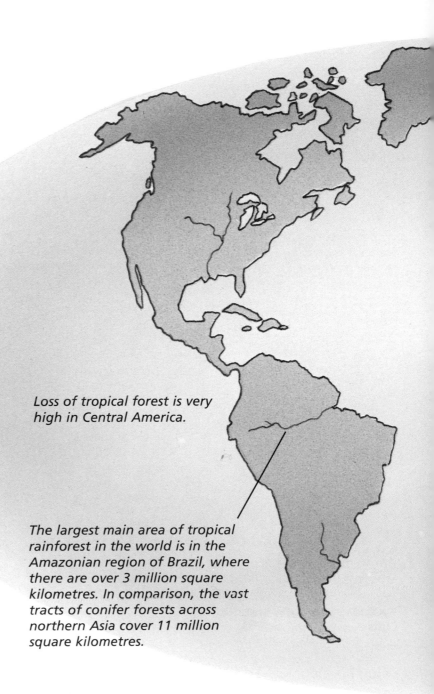

Loss of tropical forest is very high in Central America.

The largest main area of tropical rainforest in the world is in the Amazonian region of Brazil, where there are over 3 million square kilometres. In comparison, the vast tracts of conifer forests across northern Asia cover 11 million square kilometres.

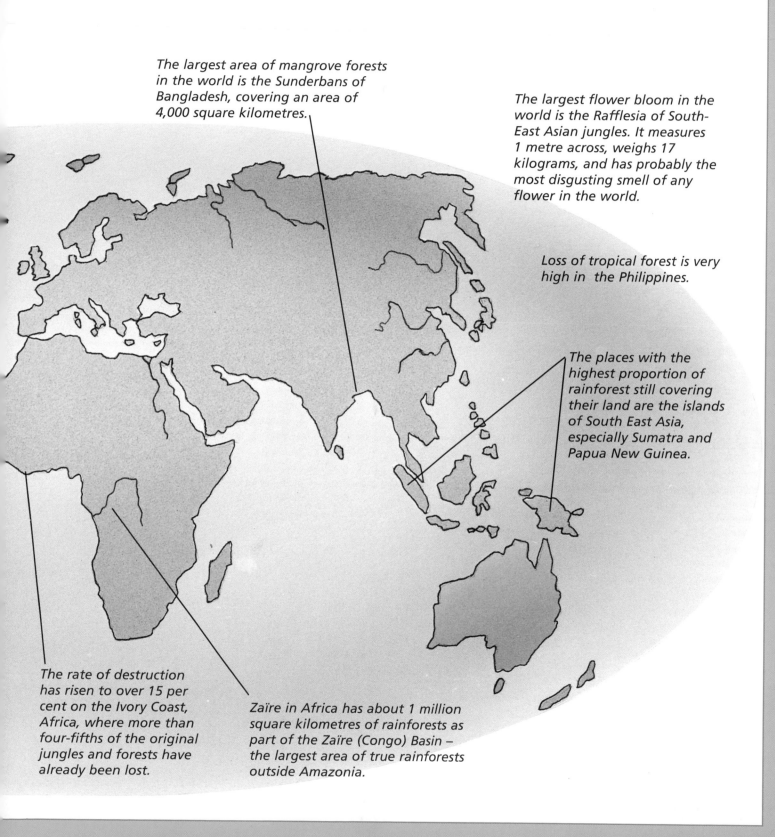

The largest area of mangrove forests in the world is the Sunderbans of Bangladesh, covering an area of 4,000 square kilometres.

The largest flower bloom in the world is the Rafflesia of South-East Asian jungles. It measures 1 metre across, weighs 17 kilograms, and has probably the most disgusting smell of any flower in the world.

Loss of tropical forest is very high in the Philippines.

The places with the highest proportion of rainforest still covering their land are the islands of South East Asia, especially Sumatra and Papua New Guinea.

The rate of destruction has risen to over 15 per cent on the Ivory Coast, Africa, where more than four-fifths of the original jungles and forests have already been lost.

Zaïre in Africa has about 1 million square kilometres of rainforests as part of the Zaïre (Congo) Basin – the largest area of true rainforests outside Amazonia.

Find Out More

There are no true rainforests in Britain, but there are many places where you can see some of the plants and animals that live in jungles and rainforests. Botanical gardens have hot-houses that reproduce the warm, moist conditions of wet tropical regions. Many common house plants, found in any garden centre come from tropical regions.

Similarly many of the exotic fruits and nuts in supermarkets come from tropical forests. Many zoos, butterfly houses and natural history museums have examples of rainforest animals.

The best organization to start with is your local County Wildlife Trust. This has details of habitats, plants and animals in your area. Ask at your library or contact The Wildlife Trusts (see below in General Information).

GENERAL INFORMATION

Forestry Commission, 231 Corstorphine Rd, Edinburgh EH12 7AT, 0131–334 0303
Institute of Terrestrial Ecology, 68 Hills Road, Cambridge CB2 1LA, 01223 69745
Open Spaces Society, 25a Bell Street, Henley-on-Thames, Oxon RG9 2BA, 014912 573535
Royal Botanic Gardens, Kew, Richmond, Surrey TW9 3AB, 0181–940 1171
Royal Botanic Gardens, Edinburgh, Scotland
The Wildlife Trusts, The Green, Witham Park, Waterside South, Lincoln LN5 7JR, 01522 544400

Zoological Society of London, Regent's Park, London NW1 4RY, 0171–722 3333

LEARNING ABOUT NATURE

Jersey Wildlife Preservation Trust, Les Augres Manor, Trinity, Jersey, Channel Islands
Amateur Entomologists' Society, 355 Hounslow Rd, Hanworth, Feltham, Middlesex TW13 5JL, 0181–755 0325
Fauna and Flora Preservation Society, 1 Kensington Gore, London, SW7 2AR, 0171–823 8899
Royal Society for the Protection of Birds (RSPB), The Lodge, Sandy, Bedfordshire SG19 2DL, 01767 680551
Wyld Court Rainforest, Hampstead Norreys, Newbury, Berkshire

HOW CAN I HELP

British Airways Assisting Conservation, 119 Grosvenor Road, Laleham Road, Staines, Middlesex TW18 2RP
British Trust for Conservation Volunteers, 36 St Mary's Street, Wallingford, Oxon OX10 OEU, 01491 39766
The Conservation Foundation, 1 Kensington Gore, London SW7 2AR, 0171–823 8842
The Earth Centre, Codicote Rd, Welwyn, Herts AL6 9TU, 01438 716478
Friends of the Earth, 26–28 Underwood St, London N1 7JQ, 0171–490 1555
Greenpeace UK, Canonbury Villas, London N1 2PN, 0171–354 5100
Wildlife Watch Trust for Environmental Education, The Green, Witham Park, Waterside South, Lincoln LN5 7JR, 01522 544400
World Land Trust, Blyth House, Bridge Street, Haleswotrth, Suffolk, 01986 874422
Worldwide Fund for Nature (WWF), Panda House, Weyside Park, Godalming, Surrey GU7 1XR, 01483 426444

BOOKS TO READ

The Amateur Naturalist Gerald Durrell, Penguin, 19
Atlas of Endangered Species editor John Burton, Macmillan, 1991
Conservation Atlases of Tropical Forests World Conservation Monitoring Centre, 219 Huntingdon Road, Cambridge CB3 0DL
The Earth and How it Works John Farndon, Dorling Kindersley
The Enchanted Canopy Andrew Mitchell, *Gorillas* Sara Godwin, Michael Friedman, 1991
The High Frontier, exploring the tropical rainforest canopy Mark W. Moffett, Harvard University Press, 1993
Our Green and Living World, The Wisdom to Save It Ayensu, Heywood, Lucas and Defilipps, Smithsonian Institution, 1984
Private Life of Plants David Attenborough, BBC Enterprises, 1995
Tropical Rainforest Arnold Newman, Facts on File, 1990

VIDEOS

The National Geographical Society and the Reader's Digest both produce a wide range of wildlife and geographical videos from around the world
BBC Natural History produces a wide range of wildlife and geographical videos, such as *David Attenborough's World of Wildlife.*

MULTIMEDIA

3D Atlas Electronic Arts, 01753 549442
A World Alive Softline, 0181–401 1234
Eyewitness Encyclopedia of Nature Dorling Kindersley, 0171–753 3488
Global Learning Mindscape, 01444 246333
Picture Atlas of the World National Geographic Society, 01483 33161
The Big Green Disk Gale Research, 01252 737630
The Environment: Land and Air Academy Television, 01532 461528
The Image of the World British Library, 0171–636 1544

Glossary

anti-coagulant A substance that stops blood clotting.

biodiversity The range and numbers of different kinds, or species, of living things.

biomass The weight of living and ex-living matter, including the plants and animals which are alive, plus their shed parts such as leaves and droppings, plus remains of animals and plants that have died and rotted.

canopy In a forest, the upper layer of branches, twigs, leaves, flowers and fruits.

carnivore An animal that eats other animals, usually a hunter that feeds on meat or flesh.

cold-blooded When an animal cannot generate much of its own internal warmth, so its body temperature varies with the temperature of its surroundings. The main cold-blooded animal groups are fish, amphibians, reptiles and all invertebrates. Compare WARM-BLOODED.

deciduous Trees that regularly lose or drop their leaves at a certain time of year, usually autumn or the dry season.

deforestation Cutting down or burning trees and clearing woodlands and forests for various uses, such as for the trees' timber, and to plant crops, raise farm animals, or build roads, factories and houses.

dormancy When a living thing remains still and inactive, as though asleep, to save energy and survive bad conditions. Aestivation and hibernation are types of dormancy.

eco-tourism When tourists, holidaymakers and sightseers visit a place to experience the natural beauties and wildlife, without damaging them too much.

evolution The gradual changes in plants, animals and other living things over long periods of time, to fit in with and survive in their changing surroundings.

habitat A type of place or surroundings in the natural world, often named after the main plants that grow there. Examples are a conifer forest, a grassland such as a meadow, a heathland, a pond or a sandy seashore. Some animals are adapted to only one habitat, like limpets on rocky seashores. Other animals, like foxes, can survive in many habitats.

herbivore An animal that eats plant food, such as shoots, stems, leaves, buds, flowers and fruits.

logging Cutting down trees for their timber or wood, to make into buildings, bridges and other structures, or for furniture, utensils and other objects.

monsoon A period or season of heavy rainfall, usually in the tropics.

open-cast mine Mining or obtaining coal, ores, minerals and other substances from the surface of the land, rather than digging underneath it.

photosynthesis 'Building with light', Catching the energy in sunlight and converting it into the energy in foods and nutrients, for living and growing. Plants are the main living things that photosynthesize.

tropics the arca of the world closest to the equator (the fattest point of the globe), defined by the northern Tropic of Cancer and the southern Tropic of Capricorn which lie 20° 30' north and south from the equator respectively

warm-blooded When an animal can generate its own internal warmth, so its body temperature is independent of the temperature of its surroundings. The main warm-blooded animal groups are mammals (including humans) and birds. Compare COLD-BLOODED.

Index